OUR SUFFICIENT GUIDE

A Study of the Bible

OUR SUFFICIENT GUIDE

A Study of the Bible

Compiled by
LILLIAN DEWATERS

OUR SUFFICIENT GUIDE

First Mystics of the World Edition 2018
ISBN: 13: 9781946362247
ISBN: 10: 1946362247

Published by Mystics of the World, Eliot, Maine
Cover graphics by Karen Leitner
Printed by CreateSpace

৵ ৵

Lillian DeWaters (1883–1964)

Originally published: 1924
Lillian DeWaters Publications
Stamford, Connecticut

CONTENTS

*It is given unto you to know the
mysteries of the kingdom of heaven.*

—*Jesus Christ*

*This gospel of the kingdom shall be
preached in all the world for a witness
unto all nations, and then shall
the end come.*

—*Jesus Christ*

Go little book, labor of love, and in His name preach the living gospel of salvation. Go, open the blind eyes, unstop the dull ears, quicken the fainting heart, waken the sleeping dead, and oh, bring the multitude to drink at the living fountain and eat of the living bread,—entering the heavenly kingdom prepared for them through the victory of Jesus Christ.

AUTHOR'S NOTES

Startling indeed are some of the truths of the Bible brought out in this compilation! Teacher, student, friend, are you a Bible student? Are you fully acquainted with the illumined word of God, and do you teach this as Truth? Do you understand the Trinity of the Godhead? Do you understand Jesus Christ? Do you understand the Holy Ghost? Read this compilation of Bible verses, topically arranged, and answer for yourself. I have used the Bible to explain the Bible, "knowing this first, that no prophecy of the scripture is of any private interpretation" (2 Pet. 1:20).

Can we easily distinguish between the imitation diamond and the real stone? There is but one method to follow in order that this be accomplished—that we make a study of the *real* stone. After one is acquainted with the real stone, then by comparison he is able to determine the value of any other stone of similar appearance.

Can dust be easily detected in a dark room? Let in the light and the dust is exposed. It is said that there are Negroes in the Far East who never knew they were black until they stood face to face with a white man. Let us take the Bible as our "real stone," as our "light," as our model and standard of Truth! As the words in this book are read, many will find themselves in a Presence they had not known before. John, the divine, said:

> If any man shall take away from the words of the book of this prophecy, if any man shall add unto these things, God shall take away his part out of the book of life and out of the holy city (Rev. 22:18-19).

9

If, in our study of books and teachers, we would feel certain whether or not it is Bible-Truth that is being taught, let us measure them by the Book of God. "If I had not come, they had not had sin," said our Master. If we are putting faith in certain doctrines and are not sufficiently acquainted with Bible-Truth to know whether that which we are believing is in accord with the teachings of Jesus Christ or not, we are in error because of our ignorance; but when Bible-Truth presents itself to us, when we see it, touch it, handle it, then our eyes are opened to behold Truth as given in the Bible and never again can we err in ignorance. The cloak of ignorance with which we might plead in the past has been stripped away. Now we stand face to face with Bible-Truth!

As we would bring a flashing white stone and lay it at the side of the real diamond to determine its value, so we do well to bring our books, our reservoir of knowledge, and lay it at the side of Truth as given in the Bible. Choose ye! You alone are to be judge for yourself, and if the Spirit "bear witness" with you, with Thomas will you exclaim, "My Lord and my God!"

Having free will, we are free to think as we like, choose as we like, teach as we like, and after our eyes are opened and we are fully acquainted with Bible-Truth, we are still free to accept it or reject it. Should we reject the facts in the Bible and neither teach them nor abide in them, how can we claim to take the Bible as our *sufficient guide*, and how can we claim to be followers of Jesus Christ?

In this compilation of Bible verses is found a clear presentation of the Trinity, or triune God; the deity of Jesus Christ—His mission, His atonement, His revealment of the Soul-Self. The reader will see what the Bible has to say about "law" and what it means to be "saved by grace."

It is also disclosed that Jesus Christ is much more than a wayshower.

The Word says, "When thou givest the wicked not warning nor speakest to warn him, the same wicked man shall die, but his blood will I require at thy hand." To him who looks and beholds and is obedient, the Word follows: "Yet, if thou warn the wicked, to save his life, and he turn not from his wickedness nor his wicked way, he shall die in his iniquity, but thou hast delivered thy soul."

What more glorious thing is there for us to do than to preach, teach, demonstrate Truth as taught in the Bible? Should we present it thus, we are still blessed whether the reader accepts or rejects it.

May the Spirit of God rest upon all who read this Bible-Truth and may Jesus Christ, Lord of lords, and King of kings, be present in your midst.

Lillian De Waters

Stamford, Conn.

WHY WE SHOULD READ
THE BIBLE

Because the inspired word of the Bible is "our suffi-cient guide" to eternal life.

There is no book with which the Bible can be com-pared, no book that can take its place. It is the standard of divine teaching.

For the prophecy came not in old time by the will of man; but holy men spake as they were moved by the Holy Ghost (2 Pet. 1:21).

All scripture is given by inspiration of God (2 Tim. 3:16).

Whereby are given unto us exceeding great and pre-cious promises (2 Pet. 1:4).

And I saw another angel fly in the midst of heaven, having the everlasting gospel to preach unto them that dwell on the earth, and to every nation, and kindred, and tongue, and people (Rev. 14:6).

Thy word is a lamp unto my feet and a light unto my path (Ps. 119:5).

THE TRINITY
(TRI-UNITY)

There are three that bear record in heaven, the Father, the Word, and the Holy Ghost: and these three are one (1 John 5:7).

Teach all nations, baptizing them in the name of the Father, and of the Son, and of the Holy Ghost (Matt. 28:19).

The angel answered and said unto her, The Holy Ghost shall come upon thee, and the power of the Highest shall overshadow thee; therefore also that holy thing which shall be born of thee shall be called the Son of God (Luke 1:35).

The Father loveth the Son, and hath given all things into his hand (John 3:35).

The Comforter, which is the Holy Ghost, whom the Father will send in my name, he shall teach you all things (John 14:26).

To us there is but one God, the Father, of whom are all things, and we in him; and one Lord Jesus Christ, by whom all things, and we by him (1 Cor. 8:6).

No man can say that Jesus is the Lord, but by the Holy Ghost (1 Cor. 12:3).

God was manifest in the flesh, justified in the Spirit, seen of angels, preached unto the Gentiles; believed on in the world, received up into glory (1Tim. 3:16).

In the beginning was the Word, and the Word was with God, and the Word was God ... And the Word was made flesh and dwelt among us (John 1:1, 14).

And his name is called the Word of God (Rev. 19:13).

THE GODHEAD

GOD, THE FATHER

HIS GREATNESS

In the beginning God created the heaven and the earth. And God saw everything that he had made, and behold, it was very good (Gen. 1:1, 31).

Thine, O Lord, is the greatness, and the power, and the glory, and the victory, and the majesty; for all that is in heaven and in the earth is thine; thine is the kingdom, O Lord, and thou art exalted as head above all (1 Chron. 29:11).

The heavens are thine, and the earth is thine; as for the world and the fullness thereof, thou hast founded them (Ps. 89:11). Before the mountains were brought forth, or ever thou hadst formed the earth, and the world, even from everlasting to everlasting, thou art God (Ps. 90:2).

How manifold are thy works! In wisdom thou hast made them all (Ps. 104:24).

Every good and every perfect gift is from above, and cometh down from the Father of lights, with whom is no variableness, neither shadow of turning (Jas. 1:17).

Who created heaven, and the things that are therein, and the earth, and the things that are therein, and the sea, and the things which are therein (Rev. 10:6).

Great and marvelous are thy works, Lord God Almighty ... all nations shall come and worship before thee (Rev. 15:3-4).

Look unto me, and be ye saved all the ends of the earth; for I am God, and there is none else (Isa. 45:22).

Can any hide himself in secret places that I shall not see him? Do not I fill heaven and earth? (Jer. 23:24).

Have we not all one Father? Hath not one God created us? (Mal. 2:10).

For there is no power but of God: the powers that be are ordained of God (Rom. 13:1). To us there is but one God, the Father, of whom are all things, and we in him (1 Cor. 8:6).

Whither shall I go from thy spirit? or whither shall I flee from thy presence? If I ascend up into heaven, thou art there: if I make my bed in hell, behold, thou art there (Ps. 139:7-8).

I know that, whatsoever God doeth, it shall be forever: nothing can be put to it, nor anything taken from it ... that which hath been is now; and that which is to be hath already been (Eccles. 3:14-15).

Before me there was no God formed, neither shall there be after me. I, even I, am the Lord; and beside me there is no Saviour (Isa. 43:10-11). I am the first, and I am the last; and beside me there is no God (Isa. 44:6).

I have made the earth, and created man upon it (Isa. 45:12).

As thou knowest not what is the way of the spirit, nor how the bones do grow in the womb of her that is with child: even so thou knowest not the works of God who maketh all (Eccles. 11:5).

The hearing ear, and the seeing eye, the Lord hath made even both of them (Prov. 20:12).

To whom will ye liken me, and make me equal, and compare me, that we may be like? ... I am God, and there is none else (Isa. 46:5, 9).

And God said unto Moses, I AM THAT I AM (Exod. 3:14).

Canst thou by searching find out God? (Job 11:7).

There is no searching of his understanding (Isa. 40:28).

To whom will ye liken God? Or what likeness will ye compare unto him? (Isa. 40:18).

Have ye not known? Have ye not heard? Hath it not been told you from the beginning? Have ye not understood from the foundations of the earth? ... Lift up your eyes on high, and behold (Isa. 40:21, 26).

Thou art my Father, my God, and the Rock of my salvation (Ps. 89:26).

The Lord he is God: it is he that hath made us, and not we ourselves (Ps. 100:3).

No man can find out the work that God maketh from the beginning to the end (Eccles. 3:11).

Touching the Almighty, we cannot find him out (Job 37:23).

His greatness is unsearchable (Ps. 145:3).

O the depth of the riches both of the wisdom and knowledge of God! How unsearchable are his judgments, and his ways past finding out! (Rom. 11:33).

The things of God knoweth no man, but the Spirit of God (1 Cor. 2:11).

Hast thou heard the secret of God? (Job 15:8).

His secret is with the righteous (Prov. 3:32).

We speak the wisdom of God in a mystery, even the hidden wisdom, which God ordained before the world unto our glory (1 Cor. 2:7).

HIS PROMISES

Ho, everyone that thirsteth, come ye to the waters, and he that hath no money; come ye, buy and eat; yea, come, buy wine and milk without money and without price (Isa. 55:1).

As I was with Moses, so I will be with thee; I will not fail thee, nor forsake thee ... Have not I commanded thee? Be strong and of a good courage; be not afraid, neither be thou dismayed: for the Lord thy God is with thee whithersoever thou goest (Josh. 1:5, 9).

When thou passest through the waters, I will be with thee ... when thou walkest through the fire, thou shalt not be burned (Isa. 43:2).

I will go before thee, and make the crooked places straight (Isa. 45:2).

Ye shall seek me, and find me, when ye shall search for me with all your heart (Jer. 29:13).

I will seek out my sheep, and will deliver them out of all places where they have been scattered in the cloudy and dark day ... And ye my flock, the flock of my pastures, are men, and I am your God (Ezek. 34:12, 31).

I will be thy King (Hos. 13:10).

Ye shall not need to fight in this battle; set yourselves, stand ye still, and see the salvation of the Lord with you (2 Chron. 20:17).

Fear ye not; for I am with thee: be not dismayed; for I am thy God: I will strengthen thee; yea, I will uphold thee with the right hand of my righteousness (Isa. 41:10).

Ye shall tread down the wicked: for they shall be ashes under the soles of your feet (Mal. 4:3).

And they shall fight against thee, but they shall not prevail against thee; for I am with thee ... to deliver thee (Jer. 1:19).

Call unto me, and I will answer thee, and show thee great and mighty things, which thou knowest not (Jer. 33:3).

I will bring the blind by a way they knew not; I will make darkness light before them (Isa.42:16).

Ye shall find rest for your souls (Jer. 6:16).

I will restore health unto thee, and I will heal thee of thy wounds (Jer. 30:17).

I will take sickness away from the midst of thee (Exod. 23:25).

I will cleanse them from all their iniquity, whereby they have sinned against me (Jer. 33:8).

I will seek that which was lost ... and will strengthen that which was sick (Ezek. 34:16).

Thou shalt not be afraid for the terror by night; nor for the arrow that flieth by day (Ps. 91:5).

I will instruct and teach thee in the way which thou shalt go (Ps. 32:8).

I, even I, am he that comforteth you (Isa. 51:12).

My presence shall go with thee, and I will give thee rest (Exod. 33:14).

No weapon that is formed against thee shall prosper; and every tongue that shall rise against thee in judgment thou shalt condemn (Isa. 54:17).

Son of man, be not afraid of them, neither be afraid of their words, though briers and thorns be with thee, and thou dost dwell among scorpions: be not afraid of their words, nor be dismayed at their looks, though they be a rebellious house ... Behold, I have made thy face strong against their faces, and thy forehead strong against their foreheads (Ezek. 2:6; 3:8).

Stand ye in the ways, and see, and ask for the old paths, where is the good way, and walk therein (Jer. 6:16). And I, the Lord thy God, will hold thy right hand, saying unto thee, Fear not, I will help thee (Isa. 41:13).

Thou shalt lay up gold as dust, and the gold of Ophir as the stones of the brooks (Job 22:24).

They that seek the Lord shall not want any good thing (Ps. 34:10).

That I may cause those that love me to inherit substance; and I will fill their treasures (Prov. 8:21).

Prove me now herewith, if I will not open you the windows of heaven, and pour you out a blessing, that there shall not be room enough to receive it (Mal. 3:10).

And they shall build houses and inhabit them; and they shall plant vineyards and eat the fruit of them (Isa. 65:21).

Ye shall not be afraid of the face of man; for the judgment is God's (Deut. 1:17).

As thy days, so shall thy strength be (Deut. 33:25).

They that wait upon the Lord shall renew their strength; they shall mount up with wings as eagles; they shall run, and not be weary; and they shall walk, and not faint (Isa.40:31).

I have loved thee with an everlasting love (Jer. 31:3).

I, even I, am he that blotteth out thy transgressions and will not remember thy sins (Isa. 43:25).

They that sow in tears shall reap in joy (Ps. 126:5).

I will turn their mourning into joy (Jer. 31:13).

Peace be unto thee; fear not; thou shalt not die (Judg. 6:23).

Fear not, for I am with thee, and will bless thee (Gen. 26:24).

There shall no evil befall thee, neither shall any plague come nigh thy dwelling (Ps. 91:10).

And my people shall dwell in a peaceable habitation, and in sure dwellings, and in quiet resting places (Isa. 32:18).

And ye shall lie down, and none shall make you afraid (Lev. 26:6).

Underneath are the everlasting arms (Deut. 33:27).

I am the Lord, the God of all flesh; is there any thing too hard for me? (Jer. 32:27).

If my people, which are called by my name, shall humble themselves, and pray, and seek my face, and turn from their wicked ways; then I will hear from heaven, and will forgive their sin, and will heal their land (2 Chron. 7:14).

Be ye strong therefore, and let not your hands be weak; for your work shall be rewarded (Isa. 65:24).

Before they call, I will answer, and while they are yet speaking, I will hear (Isa. 66:24).

I will extend peace like a river, and glory like a flowing stream (Isa. 66:12).

He shall call upon me, and I will answer him; I will be with him in trouble; I will deliver him and honor him (Ps. 91:15).

There is a path which no fowl knoweth and which the vulture's eye hath not seen (Job 28:7).

He that dwelleth in the secret place of the most High shall abide under the shadow of the Almighty ... A thousand shall fall at thy side, and ten thousand at thy right hand; but it shall not come nigh thee ... Thou shalt tread upon the lion and adder: the young lion and the dragon shalt thou trample under feet (Ps. 91:1, 7, 13).

I will walk among you, and will be your God, and ye shall be my people. I am the Lord your God, which brought you forth out of the land of Egypt ... I have broken the bands of your yoke, and made you go upright (Lev. 26:12-13).

And I will rid evil beasts out of the land, neither shall the sword go through your land (Lev. 26:6).

Be not afraid, I am with thee to deliver thee (Jer. 1:8).

Now therefore, if ye will obey my voice indeed, and keep my covenant, then ye shall be a peculiar treasure unto me above all people (Exod. 19:5).

Obey my voice, and I will be your God, and ye shall be my people (Jer. 7:23).

All the ends of the earth shall see the salvation of our God (Isa. 52:10).

Return, ye backsliding children, and I will heal your backslidings (Jer. 3:22).

I will be with thy mouth, and teach thee what thou shalt say (Exod. 4:12).

There hath not failed one word of all his good promise (1Kings 8:50).

I create new heavens and a new earth: and the former shall not be remembered, nor come into mind (Isa. 65:17).

Look unto me, and be ye saved, all the ends of the earth (Isa. 45:22).

Be still, and know that I am God (Ps. 46:10).

GOD, THE SON

HIS DEITY

In the beginning was the Word, and the Word was with God, and the Word was God ... And the Word was made flesh, and dwelt among us (John 1:1, 14).

And his name is called The Word of God (Rev. 19:13).

There are three that bear record in heaven, the Father, the Word, and the Holy Ghost (1 John 5:7).

I and my Father are one (John 10:30).

Before Abraham was, I am (John 8:58).

He that seeth me seeth him that sent me (John 12:45).

I am the way, the truth, and the life (John14:6).

Ye believe in God, believe also in me (John 14:1).

I am from above (John 8:23).

The second man is the lord from heaven (1 Cor. 15:47).

Whom do men say that I am? Whom say the people that I am? But whom say ye that I am? (Mark 8:29).

I am Alpha and Omega, the first and the last (Rev. 1:11).

Your father Abraham rejoiced to see my day; and he saw it, and was glad (John 8:56).

The voice of him that crieth in the wilderness, Prepare ye the way of the Lord, make straight in the desert a highway for our God (Isa. 40:3). This is he that was spoken of by the prophet Esaias, saying, the voice of one crying in the wilderness, Prepare ye the way of the Lord, make his paths straight (Matt. 3:3).

Lift up your heads, O ye gates ... and the King of glory shall come in. Who is this King of glory? The Lord of hosts, he is the King of glory (Ps. 24:9-10). Which none of the princes of this world knew; for had they known it, they would not have crucified the Lord of glory (1 Cor. 2:8).

Behold, the days come, saith the Lord, that I will raise unto David a righteous Branch, and a King shall reign and prosper, and shall execute judgment and justice in the earth; and this is his name whereby he shall be called, the Lord our Righteousness (Jer. 23:5-6). Of him are ye in Christ Jesus, who of God is made unto us wisdom, and righteousness, and redemption (1 Cor. 1:30).

For thou, Lord, art high above all the earth: thou art exalted far above all gods (Ps.97:9). He that cometh from above is above all ... he that cometh from heaven is above all (John 3:31).

Thus saith the Lord the King of Israel, and his redeemer the Lord of hosts; I am the first, and I am the last, and beside me there is no God (Isa. 44:6).

Hearken unto me ... I am he; I am the first, I also am the last (Isa. 48:12). I am Alpha and Omega, the beginning and the end, the first and the last (Rev. 22:13).

For by him were all things created, that are in the heaven, and that are in earth, visible and invisible ... all things were created by him, and for him ... for it pleased the Father that in him should all fullness dwell (Col. 1:16, 19). All things were made by him; and without him was not anything made that was made (John 1:3).

Of old hast thou laid the foundation of the earth ... Thou art the same, and thy years have no end (Ps. 102:25, 27). Unto the Son he saith, Thy throne, O God, is forever and ever ... thou art the same, and thy years shall not fail (Heb. 1:8, 12).

The Lord himself shall give you a sign: Behold, a virgin shall conceive, and bear a son, and shall call his name Immanuel (Isa. 7:14).

And they shall call his name Emmanuel, which being interpreted is, God is with us (Matt. 1:23).

He is Lord of lords and King of kings (Rev. 17:14).

His name shall be called Wonderful, Counseller, The mighty God, The everlasting Father, The Prince of Peace (Isa. 9:6).

That ye may know that the Son of man hath power on earth to forgive sins (Matt. 9:6).

All men should honor the Son, even as they honor the Father (John 5:23).

They saw the young child with Mary his mother, and fell down, and worshipped him (Matt. 2:11).

Behold, there came a certain ruler, and worshipped him. They came and worshipped him, saying, of a truth thou art the Son of God (Matt. 9:18).

Jesus met them, saying, All hail. And they came and held him by the feet, and worshipped him ... The disciples went into a mountain where Jesus had appointed them, and when they saw him, they worshipped him (Matt. 28:9, 16). And he led them out as far as Bethany ... and he was parted from them, and carried up into heaven. And they worshipped him (Luke 24:50-52). And let all the angels of God worship him (Heb. 1:6).

To us there is but ... one Lord Jesus Christ, by whom are all things, and we by him (1 Cor. 8:6). Who, being in the form of God, thought it not robbery to be equal with God; but took upon him the form of a servant, and was made in the likeness of men ... and became obedient ... unto the death of the cross ... That at the name of Jesus every knee should bow, of things in heaven, and things in earth, and things under the earth; *that every tongue should confess that Jesus Christ is Lord* (Phil. 2:6-11).

My Lord and my God! (John 20:28).

In him dwelleth all the fulness of the Godhead bodily (Col. 2:9).

The four beasts and four and twenty elders fell down before the Lamb ... and they sung a new song, saying, Thou art worthy to take the book, and to open the seals thereof ... Blessing, and honor, and glory, and power, be unto him that sitteth upon the throne, and unto the Lamb forever and ever. And the four and twenty elders fell down and worshipped him that liveth forever and ever (Rev. 5:8-9, 13-14).

Great is the mystery of godliness: God was manifest in the flesh (1Tim. 3:16).

The blessed and only Potentate, who knew no sin (1 Tim. 6:15).

This is the true God, and eternal life (1 John 5:20).

HIS MISSION

What think ye of Christ? (Matt. 22:42).

I am the light of the world (John 8:12). To this end was I born, and for this cause came I into the world, that I should bear witness unto the truth (John 18:37).

I am the door! ... I am the way! ... I am the bread of life! ... I am the resurrection! (John 10:9, 14; John 6:35; John 11:25).

I came not to judge the world, but to save the world (John 12:47). I am not come to call the righteous, but sinners to repentance (Matt. 9:13). For the Son of man is come to save that which was lost (Matt. 18:11).

My meat is to do the will of him that sent me, and to finish his work (John 4:34). The Son of man is not come to destroy men's lives, but to save them (Luke 9:56).

The Spirit of the Lord ... hath anointed me to preach the gospel to the poor; he hath sent me to heal the broken-hearted, to preach deliverance to the captives, and recovering of sight to the blind, to set at liberty them that are bruised ... This day is this scripture fulfilled in your ears (Luke 4:18, 21). Jesus Christ the same yesterday, and today, and forever (Heb. 13:8).

The Son of man came to minister, and to give his life a ransom for many (Mark 10:45). Who gave himself a ransom for all (1Tim. 2:6).

This is the will of him that sent me, that every one which seeth the Son, and believeth on him, may have everlasting life (John 6:40). I am come a light into the world, that whosoever believeth on me should not abide in darkness (John 12:46).

I am come to send fire on the earth ... There shall be five in one house divided, three against two, and two against three (Luke 12:49, 52).

I am come that they might have life, and that they might have it more abundantly (John 10:10).

For God so loved the world, that he gave his only begotten Son, that whosoever believeth in him should not perish, but have everlasting life (John 3:16). Thus it is written, and thus it behooved Christ to suffer, and to rise from the dead (Luke 24:46).

To this end Christ both died, and rose, and revived, that he might be Lord both of the dead and the living (Rom. 14:9) ... to redeem them that were under the law, that we might receive the adoption of sons (Gal. 4:5). This is a faithful saying, and worthy of all acceptation, that Jesus Christ came into the world to save sinners (1 Tim. 1:15). For this purpose the Son of God was manifested, that he might destroy the works of the devil (1 John 3:8).

And ye know that he was manifested to take away our sins; and in him is no sin (1 John 3:5). And we have seen and do testify that the Father sent the Son to be the Saviour of the world (John 4:14).

Men shall be blessed in him (Ps. 72:17). Thou shalt call his name *Jesus*, for he shall save his people from their sins (Matt. 1:21).

This is indeed the Christ, the Saviour of the world (John 4:42).

This is the stone which was set at naught of your builders, which is become the head of the corner (Acts 4:11). Jesus Christ himself being the chief cornerstone (Eph. 2:20). And being made perfect, he became the author of eternal salvation unto all them that obey him (Heb. 5:9).

God sent his only begotten Son into the world, that we might live through him (1 John 4:9).

Think not that I am come to destroy the law ... I am not come to destroy, but to fulfill (Matt. 5:17). Repentance and remission of sins should be preached in his name among all nations (Luke 24:47).

God sent his only begotten Son into the world ... that the world through him might be saved (John 3:17). Once in the end of the world hath he appeared to put away sin by the sacrifice of himself (Heb. 9:26).

And there was given him dominion, and glory, and a kingdom, that all people, nations, and languages, should serve him; his dominion is an everlasting dominion, which shall not pass away, and his kingdom that which shall not be destroyed (Dan. 7:14).

He shall speak peace unto the heathen: and his dominion shall be from sea even to sea, and from the river even unto the ends of the earth (Zech. 9:10).

Thou sayest that I am a king. To this end was I born (John 18:37).

HIS GIFT OF LOVE

The Free Gift

Greater love hath no man than this, that a man lay down his life for his friends (John 15:13).

God so loved the world, that he gave his only begotten Son, that whosoever believeth on him, should not perish but have everlasting life. God sent his Son into the world that the world through him might be saved (John 3:16-17).

Therefore doth my Father love me, because I lay down my life, that I might take it again ... This commandment have I received of my Father (John 10:17-18). The Son of man came not to be ministered unto, but to minister, and to give his life a ransom for many (Mark 10:45).

God sent forth his Son, made of a woman, made under the law, to redeem them that were under the law (Gal. 4:4-5). In whom we have redemption through his blood, the forgiveness of sins, according to the riches of his grace (Eph. 1:7). Christ hath redeemed us from the curse of the law, being made a curse for us (Gal. 3:13).

For there is one God, and one mediator between God and men, the man Christ Jesus, who gave himself a ransom for all (1 Tim. 2:5-6). And he is the propitiation for our sins: and not for ours only, but also for the sins of the whole world (1 John 2:2).

He was wounded for our transgressions, he was bruised for our iniquities ... with his stripes we are healed (Isa. 53:5).

As in Adam all die, even so in Christ shall all be made alive (1 Cor. 15).

Herein is love, not that we loved God, but that he loved us, and sent his Son to be a propitiation for our sins (1 John 4:10) ... who gave himself for us, that he might redeem us from all iniquity, and purify unto himself a peculiar people (Tit. 2:14) ... him that loved us, and washed us from our sins in his own blood (Rev. 1:5).

For the judgment was by one to condemnation, but the free gift is of many offences, unto justification. For if by one man's offence death reigned by one, much more they which receive abundantly of grace and of the gift of righteousness shall reign in life by one, Jesus Christ. Therefore as by the offence of one judgment came upon all men to condemnation, even so by the righteousness of one, the free gift came upon all men unto justification of life (Rom. 5:16-18).

The gift of God is eternal life through Jesus Christ our Lord (Rom. 6:23).

God was in Christ, reconciling the world unto himself (2 Cor. 5:19). And you, that were sometime alienated and enemies in your mind by wicked works, yet now hath he reconciled (Col. 1:21).

All things are of God, who hath reconciled us to himself by Jesus Christ (2 Cor. 5:18) ... that he by the grace of God should taste death for every man (Heb. 2:9). This is a faithful saying, and worthy of all acceptation, that Christ Jesus came into the world to save sinners (1 Tim. 1:15).

Hereby perceive we the love of God, because he laid down his life for us (1 John 3:16). Not by any works of righteousness which we have done, but according to his mercy he saved us (Tit. 3:5).

The preaching of the cross is to them that perish foolishness; but unto us which are saved it is the power of God (1 Cor. 1:18).

I am the living bread which came down from heaven … the bread that I will give is my flesh, which I will give for the life of the world (John 6:51).

So Christ was once offered to bear the sins of many (Heb. 9:28). The just for the unjust, that he might bring us to God (1 Pet. 3:18). There is therefore now no condemnation to them which are in Christ Jesus (Rom. 8:1).

Christ must needs have suffered and risen from the dead; and this Jesus, whom I preach unto you, is Christ (Acts 17:30). Who was delivered for our offences, and was raised again for our justification (Rom. 4:25). Who gave himself for our sins, that he might deliver us from this present evil world, according to the will of God and our Father (Gal. 1:1).

I am the good shepherd; the good shepherd giveth his life for the sheep … My sheep hear my voice, and I know them, and they follow me: and I give unto them eternal life; and they shall never perish, neither shall any man pluck them out of my hand (John 10:11, 27-28).

The works which the Father hath given me to finish, the same works that I do, bear witness of me, that the Father hath sent me (John 5:36). I am the living bread which came down from heaven; if any man eat of this bread, he shall live forever (John 6:51).

I have trodden the winepress alone; and of the people there was none with me (Isa. 63:3).

If the Son therefore shall make you free, ye shall be free indeed (John 8:36).

He became the author of eternal salvation unto all them that obey him (Heb. 5:9).

He that acknowledgeth the son hath the father also (1 John 2:23).

I bring you good tidings of great joy, which shall be to all people (Luke 2:10). For the Son of man is come to seek and to save that which was lost (Luke 19:10). God is no respecter of persons (Acts 10:34). Christ is the end of the law to everyone that believeth (Rom. 10:4).

So then faith cometh by hearing, and hearing by the word of God (Rom. 10:17). By grace are ye saved through faith; not of works, lest any man should boast (Eph. 2:8-9).

For ye were as sheep going astray; but now are returned unto the Shepherd and Bishop of your souls (1 Pet. 2:25).

If any man thirst, let him come unto me, and drink (John 7:37).

Ye believe in God, believe also in me (John 14:1).

Peace I leave with you (John 14:27).

Without me ye can do nothing (John 15:5).

HIS MINISTRY

They brought unto him all sick people that were taken with divers diseases and torments, and those which were possessed with devils, and those which were lunatic, and those that had the palsy; and he healed them (Matt. 4:24).

The Son of man came not to be ministered unto, but to minister (Matt. 20:28).

Can Satan cast out Satan? (Mark 3:23). If I cast out devils by the Spirit of God, then the kingdom of God is come unto you (Matt. 12:28).

And, behold, they brought unto him a man sick of the palsy, lying on a bed: and Jesus seeing their faith said unto the sick of the palsy: Son, be of good cheer; thy sins be forgiven thee ... Arise, take up thy bed and go unto thine house. And he arose, and departed to his house (Matt. 9:2, 6-7).

There came to him a certain man, kneeling down to him, and saying, Lord, have mercy on my son: for he is a lunatic ... I brought him to thy disciples, and they could not cure him ... And Jesus rebuked the devil; and he departed out of him; and the child was cured from that very hour (Matt. 17:14-16, 18).

There was a woman which had a spirit of infirmity eighteen years, and was bowed together, and could in no wise lift up herself. And when Jesus saw her, he called her to him, and said unto her, Woman, thou art loosed from thine infirmity. And he laid his hands on her, and immediately she was made straight, and glorified God (Luke 13:11-13).

And it came to pass, a certain blind man sat by the wayside begging ... and he cried, saying, Jesus, thou son of David, have mercy on me ... And Jesus stood, and commanded him to be brought unto him; and when he was come near, he asked him, What wilt thou that I shall do unto thee? And he said, Lord that I may receive my sight (Luke 18:35, 38, 40-41).

And Jesus said unto him, Receive thy sight: thy faith hath saved thee And immediately he received his sight, and followed him, glorifying God (Luke 18:42-43).

Our friend Lazarus sleepeth; but I go, that I may awake him out of sleep (John 11:11).

When Jesus came, he found that he had lain in the grave four days ... And Jesus lifted up his eyes, and said, Father, I thank thee that thou hast heard me. And I knew that thou hearest me always; but because of the people which stand by I said it, that they may believe that thou hast sent me ... And when he thus had spoken, he cried with a loud voice, Lazarus, come forth. And he that was dead came forth (John 11:17, 41-42).

Jesus, having loved his own which were in the world, he loved them unto the end ... he laid aside his garments; and took a towel, and girded himself. After that he poureth water into a basin and began to wash the disciples' feet, and to wipe them with the towel wherewith he was girded ... If I wash thee not, thou hast no part with me ... If I then, your Lord and Master, have washed your feet; ye also ought to wash one another's feet (John 13:1, 4-5, 8, 14).

I have compassion on the multitude. ... If I send them away fasting to their own houses, they will faint by the way ... And he commanded the people to sit down on the ground: and he took the seven loaves, and gave thanks, and brake, and gave to his disciples to set before them ...

And they had a few small fishes; and he blessed and commanded to set them also before them (Mark 8:2-3, 6-7).

So they did eat, and were filled ... And they that had eaten were about four thousand (Mark 8:8-9).

As they sailed he fell asleep; and there came down a storm of wind on the lake; and they were filled with water, and were in jeopardy ... He arose, and rebuked the wind and the raging of the water; and they ceased, and there was a calm (Luke 8:23-24).

Simon, I have prayed for thee, that thy faith fail not; and when thou art converted, strengthen thy brethren (Luke 22:32).

And he (the malefactor) said unto Jesus, Lord, remember me when thou comest into thy kingdom. And Jesus said unto him, Today shalt thou be with me in paradise (Luke 23:42-43).

A new commandment I give unto you, That ye love one another; as I have loved you, that ye also love one another (John 13:34).

When the Comforter is come, whom I will send unto you from the Father, he shall testify of me (John 15:26).

He will guide you unto all truth ... be of good cheer. I have overcome the world (John 16:13, 33).

HIS PROMISES

Come unto me, all ye that labor and are heavy laden, and I will give you rest (Matt. 11:28).

Blessed are they which do hunger and thirst after righteousness; for they shall be filled (Matt. 5:6).

I am the living bread (John 6:51). I am the resurrection (John 11:25). I am the way (John 14:6). I am the Son of God (Matt. 27:43). I am the light of the world (John 8:12). I am the truth (John 14:6).

As the living Father hath sent me, and I live by the Father; so he that eateth me, even he shall live by me. ... He that eateth of this bread shall live forever (John 6:57-58).

He that believeth on the Son hath everlasting life (John 3:36). Follow me, and I will make you fishers of men (Matt. 4:19).

Whosoever drinketh of the water that I shall give him shall never thirst; but the water that I shall give him shall be in him a well of water springing up into everlasting life (John 4:14).

God so loved the world, that he gave his only begotten Son, that whosoever believeth in him should not perish, but have everlasting life. God sent his Son into the world that the world through him might be saved (John 3:16-17).

Ask, and it shall be given you; seek, and ye shall find; knock, and it shall be opened unto you. Every one that asketh receiveth; and he that seeketh findeth; and to him that knocketh, it shall be opened (Matt. 7:7-8).

All things, whatsoever ye shall ask in prayer, believing, ye shall receive (Matt. 21:22). If ye shall ask anything in my name, I will do it (John 14:14).

What things soever ye desire, when ye pray, believe that ye receive them, and ye shall have them (Mark 11:24). If ye abide in me, and my words abide in you, ye shall ask what ye will, and it shall be done unto you (John 15:7).

In the world ye shall have tribulation; be of good cheer; I have overcome the world (John 16:33).

It is your Father's good pleasure to give you the kingdom (Luke 12:32).

Blessed are they that hear the word of God and keep it (Luke 11:28).

He that believeth on me, the works that I do, shall he do also; and greater works than these shall he do (John 14:12).

Ye shall know the truth, and the truth shall make you free (John 8:32).

Forgive, and ye shall be forgiven (Luke 6:37).

He that loveth me shall be loved of my Father, and I will love him, and will manifest myself to him (John 14:21). There shall be one fold, and one shepherd (John10:16).

The kingdom of God is within you (Luke 17:21).

Take my yoke upon you, and learn of me; for I am meek and lowly in heart; and ye shall find rest unto your souls (Matt. 11:29).

With God nothing shall be impossible (Luke 1:37).

I am the light of the world; he that followeth me shall not walk in darkness, but shall have the light of life (John 8:12). I go away, and come again unto you (John14:28).

Seek ye first the kingdom of God, and all these things shall be added unto you (Matt. 6:33). Be thou faithful unto death, and I will give thee a crown of life (Rev. 2:10).

To him that overcometh will I give to eat of the tree of life ... He that overcometh shall not be hurt of the second death ... He that overcometh, and keepeth my works unto the end, to him will I give power over the nations (Rev. 2:7, 11, 26).

Behold, I come quickly (Rev. 22:12).

Him that overcometh will I make a pillar in the temple of my God, and I will write upon him the name of my God, and the name of the city of my God ... and I will write upon him my new name (Rev. 3:12).

Behold, I stand at the door and knock; if any man hear my voice, and open the door, I will come in to him, and will sup with him, and he with me ... To him that overcometh will I grant to sit with me in my throne (Rev. 3:20-21).

God shall wipe away all tears from their eyes; and there shall be no more death, neither sorrow nor crying, neither shall there be any more pain; for the former things are passed away (Rev. 21:4).

Behold, I make all things new (Rev. 21:5).

I am the good shepherd ... My sheep hear my voice, and they follow me; and I give unto them eternal life; and they shall never perish, neither shall any man pluck them out of my hand (John 10:14, 27-28). Whosoever shall offend one of these little ones that believe in me, it is better for him that a millstone were hanged around his neck, and he were cast into the sea (Mark 9:42).

Whosoever shall give to drink unto one of these little ones a cup of cold water only in the name of a disciple, verily I say unto you, he shall in no wise lose his reward (Matt. 10:42).

Blessed are the poor in Spirit: for theirs is the kingdom of heaven. Blessed are they that mourn: for they shall be comforted. Blessed are the meek: for they shall inherit the earth. Blessed are they which do hunger and thirst after righteousness: for they shall be filled (Matt. 5:3-6).

Blessed are the merciful: for they shall obtain mercy. Blessed are the pure in heart: for they shall see God. Blessed are the peacemakers: for they shall be called the children of God. Blessed are they which are persecuted for righteousness' sake: for theirs is the kingdom of heaven. Blessed are ye, when men shall revile you, and persecute you, and shall say all manner of evil against you falsely, for my sake. Rejoice, and be exceeding glad; for great is your reward in heaven; for so persecuted they the prophets which were before you (Matt. 5:7-12).

Heaven and earth shall pass away, but my words shall not pass away (Matt. 24:35).

Him that cometh to me I will in no wise cast out (John 6:37).

He that cometh to me shall never hunger; and he that believeth on me shall never thirst … He that believeth on me hath everlasting life (John 6:35, 47).

When thou prayest, enter into thy closet, and when thou hast shut thy door, pray to thy Father which is in secret; and thy Father which seeth in secret shall reward thee openly (Matt. 6:6).

Behold, I give unto you power to tread on serpents and scorpions; and over all the power of the enemy; and nothing shall by any means hurt you (Luke 10:19).

These signs shall follow them that believe; in my name shall they cast out devils; they shall speak with new tongues. They shall take up serpents; and if they drink any deadly thing, it shall not hurt them; they shall lay hands on the sick, and they shall recover (Mark 16:17-18).

Verily I say unto you, that whosoever shall say unto this mountain, Be thou removed, and be thou cast into the sea; and shall not doubt in his heart, but shall believe that those things which he saith shall come to pass; he shall have whatsoever he saith (Mark 11:23).

My grace is sufficient for thee; for my strength is made perfect in weakness (2 Cor. 12:9). I will give you a mouth and wisdom which all your adversaries shall not be able to gainsay nor resist (Luke 21:15).

In my Father's house are many mansions ... I go to prepare a place for you, that where I am, there ye may be also ... Peace I leave with you, my peace I give unto you ... I will come again, and will receive you unto myself; that where I am, there ye may be also (John 14:2-3, 27).

I will never leave thee nor forsake thee (Heb. 13:5).

As Moses lifted up the serpent in the wilderness, even so must the Son of man be lifted up (John 3:14). I, if I be lifted up from the earth, will draw all men unto me (John 12:32).

I will not leave you comfortless; I will come to you (John 14:18).

If I go not away, the Comforter will not come unto you; but if I depart, I will send him unto you; and when he is come, he will reprove the world of sin ... When he, the Spirit of truth, is come, he will guide you into all truth ... He shall glorify me: for he shall receive of mine, and shall show it unto you. All things that the Father hath are mine (John 16:7-8, 13-15).

Be not afraid (John 6:20). Be of good cheer; I have overcome the world (John 16:33).

Behold, I come quickly; blessed is he that keepeth the sayings of the prophecy of this book (Rev. 22:7).

Let him that is athirst come (Rev. 22:17).

Lo, I am with you alway, even unto the end of the world (Matt. 28:20).

HIS VICTORY

All hail! ... It is finished! ... Behold your King! (Matt. 28; John 19:30; John 19:14).

And this is the record, that God hath given to us eternal life, and this life is in his Son (1 John 5:11).

I am the resurrection ... I am the life (John 11:25).

Let not your heart be troubled (John 14:1). I have overcome the world (John 16:33).

The hour is come (John 17:1). By man came death, by man came also the resurrection of the dead (1 Cor. 15:21). He that hath the Son hath life; and he that hath not the Son of God hath not life (1 John 5:12).

The cup my Father hath given me, shall I not drink it? (John 18:11, 37). To this end was I born, and for this cause came I into the world, that I should bear witness unto the truth. Your father Abraham rejoiced to see my day (John 8:56).

And we know that the Son of God is come, and hath given us an understanding, that we may know him that is true, and we are in him that is true, even in his Son Jesus Christ. This is the true God and eternal life (1 John 5:20).

Be of good cheer (John 16:33). No man cometh unto the Father but by me (John 14:6). I am he that liveth, and was dead; and, behold, I am alive for evermore (Rev. 1:18).

Ye shall receive power, after that the Holy Ghost is come upon you (Acts 1:8). Go ye therefore, and teach all nations, baptizing them in the name of the Father, and of the Son, and of the Holy Ghost (Matt. 28:19).

Lo, I am with you alway, even unto the end of the world (Matt. 28:20). Jesus Christ the same yesterday, and today, and forever (Heb. 13:8).

If Christ be not risen, then is our preaching vain, and your faith is also vain (1 Cor. 15:14). In him dwelleth all the fulness of the Godhead bodily (Col. 2:9).

And the glory which thou gavest me, I have given them (John 17:22). All mine are thine, and thine are mine ... that they all may be one; as thou, Father, art in me, and I in thee, that they also may be one in us; that the world may believe that thou hast sent me (John 10:21).

If ye then be risen with Christ, seek those things which are above (1 Col. 3:1).

If the Spirit that raised up Jesus from the dead dwell in you, he that raised up Christ from the dead shall also quicken your mortal bodies by his Spirit that dwelleth in you (Rom. 8:1). As the Father raiseth up the dead, and quickeneth them; even so the Son quickeneth whom he will (John 5:21).

We see Jesus ... crowned with glory and honor; that through death he might destroy him that had the power of death, that is, the devil (Heb. 2:9, 14).

O death, where is thy sting? O grave, where is thy victory? ... Death is swallowed up in victory (1 Cor. 15:54-55).

When he ascended up on high, he led captivity captive (Eph. 4:8).

I have the keys of hell and death (Rev.1:18).

Behold, I make all things new (Rev. 21:5).

All power is given unto me in heaven and in earth (Matt. 28:18).

I will give unto him that is athirst of the fountain of the water of life freely (Rev. 21:6).

Now is the Son of man glorified, and God is glorified in him (John 13:31).

The God of our fathers raised up Jesus ... and exalted him to be a Prince and a Saviour (Acts 5:30-31). Ye are complete in him, which is the head of all principality and power (Col. 2:10).

All nations shall call him blessed (Ps. 72:17).

Blessed be the Lord God of Israel; for he hath visited and redeemed his people (Luke 1:68). This is the stone which is become the head of the corner (Acts 4:11).

It is done! I am Alpha and Omega, the beginning and the end (Rev. 21:6).

Worthy is the Lamb that was slain to receive power, and riches, and wisdom, and strength, and honor, and glory, and blessing ... Blessing, and honor, and glory, and power, be unto him that sitteth upon the throne, and unto the Lamb forever and ever (Rev. 5:12-13).

And they sing the song of Moses, and the song of the Lamb, saying, Great and marvelous are thy works, Lord God Almighty ... Who shall not glorify thy name? For thou only art holy: for all nations shall come and worship before thee (Rev. 15:3-4).

And his name is called The Word of God (Rev. 19:13).

COME!

GOD, THE HOLY GHOST

GOD, THE HOLY GHOST

Have ye received the Holy Ghost since ye believed? (Acts 19:2).

How shall we escape, if we neglect so great salvation? (Heb. 2:3).

The Comforter, which is the Holy Ghost, whom the Father will send in my name, he shall teach you all things (John 14:26). When the Comforter is come, he shall testify of me (John 15:26).

Go ye therefore, and teach all nations, baptizing them in the name of the Father, and of the Son, and of the Holy Ghost (Matt. 28:19). Take ye no thought how or what thing ye shall say: for the Holy Ghost shall teach you in the same hour what ye ought to say (Luke 12:11-12).

And Jesus, when he was baptized, went up straightway out of the water; and lo, the heavens were opened unto him, and he saw the Spirit of God descending like a dove, and lighting upon him; and lo, a voice from heaven saying, This is my beloved Son, in whom I am well pleased (Matt. 3:16-17).

And as he prayed, the fashion of his countenance was altered, and his raiment was white and glistening ... and his face did shine as the sun, and his raiment was white as the light (Luke 9:29). While he yet spake, behold, a bright cloud overshadowed them: and behold a voice out of the cloud, which said, This is my beloved Son, in whom I am well pleased; hear ye him (Matt. 17:2, 5).

It is expedient for you that I go away; for if I go not away, the Comforter will not come unto you; but if I depart, I will send him unto you ... Howbeit, when he, the

Spirit of truth is come, he will guide you into all truth ...
he shall glorify me (John 16:7, 13-14).

John truly baptized with water; but ye shall be baptized with the Holy Ghost not many days hence ... Ye
shall receive power, after the Holy Ghost is come upon
you (Acts 1:5, 8).

And when the day of Pentecost was fully come, they
were all with one accord in one place. And suddenly there
came a sound from heaven as of a rushing mighty wind,
and it filled all the house where they were sitting. And
there appeared unto them cloven tongues like as of fire,
and it sat upon each of them. And they were all filled with
the Holy Ghost, and began to speak with other tongues, as
the Spirit gave them utterance (Acts 2:1-4).

Then said Peter unto them, Repent, and be baptized
every one of you in the name of Jesus Christ for the
remission of sins, and ye shall receive the gift of the Holy
Ghost ... and the same day there were added unto them
about three thousand souls (Acts 2:38, 41).

The Kingdom of God is righteousness, and peace,
and joy in the Holy Ghost (Rom. 4:17).

Desire spiritual gifts, but rather that ye may prophesy.
For he that speaketh in an unknown tongue speaketh not
unto men, but unto God; for no man understandeth him;
howbeit in the Spirit he speaketh mysteries. But he that
prophesieth speaketh unto men to edification, and exhor-
tion, and comfort. He that speaketh in an unknown tongue
edifieth himself; but he that prophesieth edifieth the church
... Greater is he that prophesieth than he that speaketh
with tongues, except he interpret (1 Cor. 14:1-5).

For our gospel came not unto you in word only, but
also in power, and in the Holy Ghost (1Thess. 1:5).

No prophecy of the scripture is of any private interpretation; for the prophecy came not in old time by the will of man; but holy men of God spake as they were moved by the Holy Ghost (2 Pet. 1:20-21).

I will pray the Father, and he shall give you another Comforter, that he may abide with you forever ... He dwelleth with you ... he shall teach you all things (John 14:16-17, 26).

How much more shall your heavenly Father give the Holy Spirit to them that ask him? (Luke 11:3). The kingdom of God is not in word, but in power, and in the Holy Ghost (1 Thess. 1:5).

The Spirit is truth (1 John 5:6). It is the Spirit that quickeneth (John 6:63). Eye hath not seen ... the things which God hath prepared, but God hath revealed them unto us by his Spirit; for the Spirit searcheth all things, yea, the deep things of God (1 Cor. 2:9-10) ... through mighty signs and wonders, by the power and the Spirit of God (Rom. 15:19).

To one is given by the Spirit the word of wisdom ... to another faith by the same Spirit; to another gifts of healing by the same Spirit; to another the working of miracles ... to another tongues; to another interpretation of tongues. All these worketh that one and the selfsame Spirit ... We are all baptized into one body, and all made to drink into one Spirit (1 Cor. 12:8-13).

Happy are ye ... for the Spirit of glory and of God resteth upon you (1 Pet. 3:14; 1 Pet. 4:14).

There are three that bear record in heaven, the Father, the Word, and the Holy Ghost; these three are one (1 John 5:7).

And he commanded us to preach unto the people ... that through his name whosoever believeth in him shall receive remission of sins. While Peter yet spake these words, the Holy Ghost fell on all them that heard the word (Acts 10:42-44).

When Paul laid his hands upon them, the Holy Ghost came on them; and they spake with tongues and prophesied (Acts 19:6) … God bearing witness, both with signs and wonders, and with divers miracles, and gifts of the Holy Ghost (Heb. 2:4).

Repent, and be baptized every one of you in the name of Jesus Christ … and ye shall receive the gift of the Holy Ghost. The promise is unto you, and to your children, and to all that are afar off (Acts. 2:38-39).

But ye, beloved, building up yourselves on your most holy faith, praying in the Holy Ghost, keep yourselves in the love of God (Jude 20-21).

SAVED BY GRACE

I am the way (John 14:6).

He that believeth on me, out of his belly shall flow rivers of living water (John 7:3) If thou canst believe, all things are possible to him that believeth (Mark. 9:23).

As Moses lifted up the serpent in the wilderness, even so must the Son of man be lifted up (John 3:14). No man can come to me, except the Father which hath sent me draw him (John 6:44). I, if I be lifted up, will draw all men unto me (John 12:32).

All have sinned, and come short of the glory of God … being justified freely by his grace through the redemption that is in Christ Jesus (Rom. 3:23-24).

By grace are ye saved through faith; and that not of yourselves; it is the gift of God … God commendeth his love toward us, in that, while we were yet sinners, Christ died for us (Eph. 2:8). If through the offence of one many be dead, much more the grace of God, and the gift by grace, which is by one man, Jesus Christ, hath abounded unto many ((Rom. 5:8, 15).

Where sin abounded, grace did much more abound; that as sin hath reigned unto death, even so might grace reign through righteousness unto eternal life by Jesus Christ our Lord (Rom. 6:21-22). Being justified by his grace, we should be made heirs according to the hope of eternal life (Tit. 3:7).

Jesus Christ, who hath saved us, and called us with an holy calling, not according to our works, but according to his own purpose and grace (2 Tim. 1:9). Not he that commendeth himself is approved, but whom the Lord commendeth (2 Cor. 10:18).

Let us therefore come boldly unto the throne of grace, that we may obtain mercy, and find grace to help in time of need (Heb. 4:16). Unto him that loved us, and washed us from our sins in his own blood, and hath made us kings and priests unto God ... to him be glory forever and ever (Rev. 1:5-6).

Unto every one of us is given grace according to the measure of the gift of Christ (Eph. 4:7).

If we confess our sins, he is faithful and just to forgive us our sins, and to cleanse us from all unrighteousness (1 John 1:9). God, who is rich in mercy, for his great love wherewith he loved us, even when we were dead in sins, hath quickened us together with Christ, (by grace ye are saved) (Eph. 2:4-5).

How beautiful upon the mountains are the feet of him that bringeth good tidings; that publisheth salvation (Isa. 52:7).

Thanks be unto God for his unspeakable gift (2 Cor. 9:15).

I am not ashamed of the gospel of Christ; for it is the power of God unto salvation to everyone that believeth (Rom. 1:16). Not by might, nor by power, but by my spirit, saith the Lord (Zech. 4:6).

Jesus said unto the disciples, If a man will come after me, let him deny himself, and take up his cross, and follow me (Matt. 16:24). For whosoever will save his life shall lose it; but whosoever will lose his life for my sake shall find it (Mark 8:35).

For this cause I bow my knees unto the Father of our Lord Jesus Christ ... That Christ may dwell in your hearts by faith; that ye, being rooted and grounded in love, may be able to comprehend and to know the love of Christ, which passeth knowledge, that ye might be filled with all the fulness of God (Eph. 3:14, 17, 19).

Today, if ye will hear his voice, harden not your hearts (Heb. 3:7-8).

Stand fast therefore in the liberty wherewith Christ hath made us free, and be not entangled again in the yoke of bondage (Gal. 5:1).

If any man be in Christ, he is a new creature (2 Cor. 5:17). Christ in you the hope of glory (Col. 1:27). If ye then be risen with Christ, seek those things which are above (Col. 3:1). Whosoever abideth in him, sinneth not (1 John 3:6). Greater is he that is in you, than he that is in the world (John 4:4).

He that abideth in the doctrine of Christ, he hath both the Father and the Son (2 John 1:9).

Put ye on the Lord Jesus Christ (Rom. 13:14). As many of you as have been baptized into Christ, have put on Christ (Gal. 3:27).

This is the victory that overcometh the world, even our faith. We know that the Son of God is come, and hath given us an understanding, that we may know him that is true, and we are in him that is true, even in his Son Jesus Christ (1 John 5:4, 20).

Put on therefore ... humbleness of mind, meekness (Col. 3:12). With the lowly is wisdom (Prov. 11:2). Be not high-minded ... lest ye be should wise in your own conceits (Rom. 11:20, 25). For I say to every man not to think of himself more highly than he ought to think (Rom. 12:3). Let him that thinketh he standeth, take heed lest he fall (1 Cor. 10:12). God forbid that I should glory, save in the cross of our Lord Jesus Christ (Gal. 6:14).

They sought it not by faith, but as it were by the works of the law, for they stumbled at that stumbling-stone (Rom. 9:32). If it be of works, then it is no more grace (Rom. 11:6). After ye have known God, or rather are known of God, how turn ye again to the weak and beggarly elements, whereunto ye desire again to be in bondage? (Gal. 4:9).

If ye be led of the Spirit, ye are not under the law (Gal. 5:18).

Not by works of righteousness which we have done, but according to his mercy he saved us (Tit. 3:5).

One soweth and another reapeth. I sent you to reap that whereon ye bestowed no labor (John 4:37-38). Lift up your eyes and look on the fields; for they are white already to harvest (John 10:9).

Whoso looketh into the perfect law of liberty, and continueth therein ... shall be blessed (Jas. 1:25).

My grace is sufficient for thee; for my strength is made perfect in weakness (2 Cor. 12:9).

I am the door (John 14:6).

There is none other name given among men, whereby we must be saved (Acts 4:12).

He hath not dealt with us after our sins; nor rewarded us according to our iniquities ... As far as the east is from the west, so far hath he removed our transgressions from us (Ps. 103:10, 12).

Behold, now is the accepted time; now is the day of salvation (2 Cor. 6:2).

The just shall live by faith (Heb. 10:38). The fruit of the Spirit is ... faith (Gal. 5:22).

Christ is become of no effect unto you, whosoever of you are justified by the law; ye are fallen from grace (Gal. 5:4).

Faith is the substance of things hoped for ... Without faith it is impossible to please him; for he that cometh to God must believe that he is (Heb. 11:1, 6).

Concerning the work of my hands command ye me (Isa. 45:11).

Look unto me, and be ye saved, all the ends of the earth (Isa. 45:22).

They sing the song of Moses ... and the song of the Lamb (Rev. 15:3).

Except ye be converted, and become as little children, ye shall not enter into the kingdom of heaven (Matt. 18:3). I am the door; by me if any man enter in, he shall be saved, and shall go in and out, and find pasture (John 10:9). All the promises of God in him are yea, and in him Amen (2 Cor. 1:20). Faithful is he that calleth you, who also will do it (1 Thess. 5:24).

Our sufficiency is of God (2 Cor. 3:5). Every good and every perfect gift is from above (Jas. 1:27). Whereby are given unto us exceeding great and precious promises; that by these ye might be partakers of the divine nature (2 Pet. 1:4).

Come hither, and hear the words of the Lord your God (Josh. 3:9). The word of God is quick, and powerful, and sharper than any two-edged sword (Heb. 4:12). We speak ... not the wisdom of this world, but we speak the wisdom of God in a mystery, even the hidden wisdom, which God ordained before the world unto our glory (1 Cor. 2:6-7) ... the mystery, which from the beginning of the world hath been hid in God (Eph. 3:9).

This is the true grace of God (1 Pet. 5:12).

Do ye now believeth? (Col. 1:26).

The mystery which hath been hid from ages and from generations, but now is made manifest to his saints (Col. 1:26).

He that is of God heareth God's words (John 8:47).

Ye are bought with a price (1 Cor. 6:20). God was in Christ, reconciling the world unto himself (2 Cor. 5:19).

Other foundation can no man lay than that is laid, which is Jesus Christ (1 Cor. 3:11).

LAW VERSUS LOVE

Verily, verily, I say unto thee, except a man be born of water and of the Spirit, he cannot enter into the kingdom of God (John 3:5).

The baptism of John, was it from heaven, or of men? (Luke 20:4).

John truly baptized with water (Acts 1:5).

The law and the prophets were until John: since that time the kingdom of God is preached (Luke 16:16).

Think not that I am come to destroy the law, or the prophets: I am not come to destroy, but to fulfill (Matt. 5:17).

Your fathers did eat manna in the wilderness, and are dead (John 6:49).

Moses gave you not that bread from heaven ... The bread of God is he which cometh down from heaven, and giveth life unto the world: he that eateth of this bread shall live forever ... I am the bread of life (John 6:32-33, 35).

Labor not for the meat which perisheth, but for that meat which endureth unto everlasting life ... I am the living bread which came down from heaven (John 6:27, 51).

This is life eternal, that they might know thee, the only true God, and Jesus Christ, whom thou hast sent (John 17:3).

No man cometh unto the Father, but by me (John 14:6).

It is the Spirit that quickeneth (John 6:63).

Render unto Caesar the things which be Caesar's, and unto God the things which be God's (Luke 20:25).

I had not known sin, but by the law (Rom. 7:7).

The law is not made for a righteous man, but for the lawless and disobedient, for the ungodly, and for sinners, for unholy and profane, for murderers of fathers and murderers of mothers, for manslayers, for whoremongers, for them that defile themselves with mankind, for menstealers; for liars, for perjured persons, and if there be any other thing that is contrary to sound doctrine (1Tim. 1:9-10).

It is easier for heaven and earth to pass, than one tittle of the law to fail (Luke 16:17).

Whosoever committeth sin transgresseth also the law: for sin is the transgression of the law (1 John 3:4).

The motions of sins, which were by the law, did work in our members to bring forth fruit unto death (Rom. 7:5).

I am the resurrection and the life (John 11:25).

The law was given by Moses, but grace and truth came by Jesus Christ (John 1:17).

Christ is the end of the law (Rom. 10:4).

Ye blind guides, which strain at a gnat, and swallow a camel (Matt. 23:24).

Except ye be converted, and become as little children, ye shall not enter into the kingdom of heaven (Matt. 18:3).

Except a man be born again, he cannot see the kingdom of God (John 3:3).

For what the law could do, in that it was weak through the flesh, God sending his own Son in the likeness of sinful flesh, and for sin, condemned sin in the flesh (Rom. 8:3).

I am the door (John 10:7).

For God so loved the world, that he gave his only begotten Son, that whosoever believeth on him should not perish, but have everlasting life (John 3:16).

Cast out the bondwoman and her son: for the son of the bondwoman shall not be heir with the son of the freewoman. So then, brethren, we are not children of the bondwoman, but of the free (Gal. 4:30-31).

Now in Christ Jesus is our peace, who hath broken down the middle wall of partition between us, having abolished in his flesh the enmity, even the law of commandments contained in ordinances (Eph. 2:14-15).

And for this cause he is a mediator of the new testament (Heb. 9:15). For the law having a shadow of good things to come, and not the very image of the things, can never make the corners thereunto perfect … This is the covenant that I will make with them, saith the Lord, I will put my laws into their hearts, and in their minds will I write them (Heb. 10:1, 16).

I am the way … no man cometh unto the father, but by me (John 14:6).

I have overcome the world (John 16:33).

Not by works of righteousness which we have done, but according to his mercy he saved us (Tit. 3:5).

For the Son of man is come to save that which was lost (Matt. 18:11).

Who shall separate us from the love of Christ? Shall tribulation, or distress, or persecution … or peril, or sword? Nay, in all these things we are more than conquerors through him that loved us (Rom. 8:35, 37).

My little children, let us not love in word, neither in tongue; but in deed and in truth (1 John 3:18).

Thou shalt love the Lord thy God with all thy heart, and with all thy soul, and with all thy mind, and with all thy strength (Mark. 12:30).

God hath not given us the spirit of fear; but of power, and of love, and of a sound mind (2 Tim. 1:7).

Let us love one another: for love is of God (1 John 4:7).

Whosoever believeth that Jesus is the Christ is born of God (1 John 5:1).

The law worketh wrath; for where no law is, there is no transgression (Rom. 4:15).

Search the scriptures ... If we love one another, God dwelleth in us (1 John 4:12).

He that ministereth to you the Spirit, and worketh miracles among you, doeth he it by the works of the law, or by the hearing of faith? (Gal. 3:5).

They which be of faith are blessed with faithful Abraham. As many as are of the works of the law are under the curse; for it is written, Cursed is every one that continueth not in all things which are written in the book of the law to do them. But that no man is justified by the law in the sight of God, it is evident ... *The law is not of faith* ... Christ hath redeemed us from the curse of the law (Gal. 3:9-13).

Before faith came we were kept under the law, wherefore the law was our schoolmaster to bring us unto Christ, that we might be justified by faith. But after faith is come, we are no longer under a schoolmaster. For ye are all children of God by faith in Jesus Christ (Gal. 3:23-26).

Tell me, ye that desire to be under the law, do ye not hear the law? For it is written, that Abraham had two sons, the one by a bondmaid, the other by a freewoman. He who was of the bondwoman was born after the flesh; but he of the freewoman was by promise. Cast out the bondwoman and her child (Gal. 4:21-22, 30).

For by grace are ye saved through faith; and that not of yourselves: it is the gift of God (Eph. 2:8).

For the law made nothing perfect (Heb. 7:19).

But God sent forth his Son, to redeem them that were under the law (Gal. 4:4-5).

If ye be led of the Spirit, ye are not under the law (Gal. 5:18).

Stand fast therefore in the liberty wherewith Christ hath made us free, and be not entangled again with the yoke of bondage (Gal. 5:1).

Love is the fulfilling of the law (Rom. 13:10).

For what is a man profited, if he shall gain the whole world, and lose his own soul? (Matt. 16:26).

I seek not mine own glory (John 8:50) ... not having mine own righteousness, which is of the law (Phil. 3:9).

They that take the sword shall perish with the sword (Matt. 26:52). He that killeth with the sword must be killed with the sword (Rev. 13:10).

Enter ye in at the strait gate (Matt. 7:13).

The disciple is not above his master (Luke 6:40).
He that denieth me before men shall be denied before the angels of God (Luke 12:9).

He that leadeth into captivity shall go into captivity (Rev. 13:10).

Let him that glorieth glory in this, that he understandeth and knoweth me (Jer. 9:24). He that glorieth, let him glory in the Lord (2 Cor. 10:17).

Blessed are the meek: for they shall inherit the earth (Matt. 5:5).

If any man desire to be first, the same shall be last of all, and servant of all (Mark 9:35).

One is your Master, even Christ (Matt. 23:8).

If ye know these things, happy are ye if ye do them (John 13:17).

Whosoever shall not receive the kingdom of God as a little child, he shall not enter therein (Mark 10:15).

Submit yourselves therefore to God. Draw nigh to God, and he will draw nigh to you. Humble yourselves in the sight of the Lord, and he shall lift you up (Jas. 4:7-8, 10).

I am the way (John 14:6). Follow me (John 1:43).

67

While one saith, I am of Paul; and another, I am of Apollos; are ye not carnal? I have planted, Apollos watered; but God gave the increase. So then neither is he that planteth anything, neither he that watereth; but God that giveth the increase (1 Cor. 3:4, 6-7).

I am dead to the law, that I might live unto God (Gal. 2:19).

Whosoever shall exalt himself shall be abased (Matt. 23:12). No man can serve two masters (Matt. 6:24). If the blind lead the blind, both shall fall into the ditch (Matt. 15:14).

If any man have ears to hear, let him hear (Mark 4:23).

What things soever the law saith, it saith to them who are under the law … By the law is the knowledge of sin (Rom. 3:19-20).

Christ is become of no effect unto you, whosoever of you are justified by the law (Gal. 5:4).

Who hath bewitched you, that ye should not obey the truth? (Gal. 3:1).

A man is justified by faith without the deeds of the law (Rom. 3:28).

To him that worketh is the reward not reckoned of grace, but of debt; but to him that worketh not … his faith is counted for righteousness (Rom. 4:4-5).

Wherefore then serveth the law? It was added because of transgressions, till the seed should come to whom the promise was made (Gal. 3:19).

We ought to obey God rather than men (Acts 5:29).

Who did hinder you that ye should not obey the truth? (Gal. 5:7).

Whosoever abideth not in the doctrine of Christ, hath not God (2 John 1:9).

The natural man receiveth not the things of the Spirit of God (1 Cor. 2:14).

Awake thou that sleepest, and arise from the dead, and Christ shall give thee light (Eph. 5:14).

Put on the new man, which is created in righteousness and true holiness (Eph. 4:24).

The law of the Spirit of life in Christ Jesus hath made me free from the law of sin and death (Rom. 8:2).

Take ye no thought what ye shall say. The Holy Ghost shall teach you what ye ought to say (Luke 12:11-12).

O ye of little faith, why reason ye? (Matt. 16:18). Though we walk in the flesh, we do not war after the flesh (2 Cor. 10:3).

Do ye look on things after the outward appearance? (2 Cor. 10:7).

Watch and pray (Mark 13:33).

In such an hour as ye think not, the Son of man cometh (Matt. 24:44).

What I say unto you I say unto all, Watch (Mark 13:37).

MORTALS AND IMMORTALS

Children of Flesh and
Children of God

There went up a mist from the earth, and watered the whole face of the ground ... And man became a living soul (Gen. 2:6-7).

Man that is born of a woman is of few days and full of trouble (Job 14:1).

And ye have done worse than your fathers: for behold, ye walk every one after the imagination of his evil heart, that they may not hearken unto me (Jer. 16:12). Destruction and misery are in their ways (Rom. 3:16).

They which are the children of the flesh, these are not the children of God (Rom. 9:8).

Ever learning, and never able to come to the knowledge of the truth (2 Tim. 3:7). There is none righteous, no, not one (Rom. 3:10).

The natural man receiveth not the things of the Spirit of God: for they are foolishness unto him: neither can he know them, because they are spiritually discerned (1 Cor. 2:14).

Ye are yet carnal: for whereas there is among you envying, and strife, and divisions, are ye not carnal? (1 Cor. 3:3)

Whosoever doeth not righteousness is not of God, neither he that loveth not his brother (1 John 3:10).

Thou sayest, I am rich, and increased with goods, and have need of nothing; and knowest not that thou art wretched, and miserable, and poor, and blind, and naked (Rev. 3:17).

They are all gone out of the way; they are together become unprofitable; there is none that doeth good, no, not one ... For all have sinned, and come short of the glory of God (Rom. 3:12, 23).

That which is born of the flesh is flesh (John 3:6).

The wages of sin is death (Rom. 6:23). And sin, when it is finished, bringeth forth death (Jas. 1:15). If we say that we have no sin, we deceive ourselves, and the truth is not in us (1 John 1:8).

As many as are of the works of the law are under the curse (Gal. 3:10).

Ye must be born again (John 3:7).

It is your Father's good pleasure to give you the kingdom (Luke 12:32).

I will arise and go to my father (Luke 15:18).

Except a corn of wheat fall into the ground and die, it abideth alone; but if it die, it bringeth forth much fruit (John 12:24).

Learn of me (Matt. 11:29). If any man will come after me, let him deny himself, and take up his cross, and follow me (Matt. 15:24). We ought to lay down our lives for the brethren (1 John 3:16).

As we have borne the image of the earthy, we shall also bear the image of the heavenly (1 Cor. 15:49).

Verily, I say unto thee, except a man be born of water and of the Spirit, he cannot enter into the kingdom of God (John 3:5).

As many as received him, to them gave he power to become the sons of God (John 1:12).

As many as are led by the Spirit of God, they are the sons of God ... Ye have received the spirit of adoption, whereby we cry, Abba, Father. The Spirit itself beareth witness with our spirit, that we are the children of God ... heirs of God, and joint-heirs with Christ (Rom. 8:14-17).

The children of the promise are counted for the seed (Rom. 9:8).

Wherefore come out from among them, and be ye separate, saith the Lord ... and I will receive you ... and ye shall be my sons and daughters, saith the Lord Almighty (2 Cor. 6:17-18).

Ye are all the children of God by faith in Jesus Christ ... and heirs according to the promise (Gal. 3:36, 29). And because ye are sons, God hath sent forth the Spirit of his Son into your hearts (Gal. 4:6).

That ye may be blameless and harmless, the sons of God, without rebuke, in the midst of a crooked and perverse nation, among whom ye shine as lights in the world (Phil. 2:15).

The Lord scourgeth every son whom he receiveth. If ye endure chastening, God dealeth with you as with sons; for what son is he whom the father chasteneth not? (Heb. 12:6-7).

We all are changed ... from glory to glory (2 Cor. 3:18).

Behold, what manner of love the Father hath bestowed upon us, that we should be called the sons of God ... Beloved, now we are the sons of God (1 John 3:1-2).

He that overcometh shall inherit all things; and I will be his God, and he shall be my son (Rev. 21:7).

By man came also the resurrection of the dead ... in Christ shall all be made alive (1 Cor. 15:21-22).

There is neither Jew nor Greek, there is neither bond nor free, there is neither male nor female; for ye are all one in Christ Jesus (Gal. 3:28).

That which is born of the Spirit is spirit (John 3:6).

Being born again ... by the word of God, which liveth
and abideth forever (1 Pet. 1:23).

JOY

Let all those that put their trust in thee, rejoice; let them shout for joy (Ps. 5:11).

In thy presence is fulness of joy; at thy right hand there are pleasures for evermore (Ps. 16:11).

The Lord thy God in the midst of thee is mighty; he will save, he will rejoice over thee with joy, he will joy over thee with singing (Zeph. 3:17).

God giveth to a man that is good in his sight, joy (Eccles. 2:26).

Enter thou into the joy of thy Lord (Matt. 25:23).

I have no greater joy than to hear that my children walk in truth (3 John 1:4).

Count it all joy when ye fall into diverse temptations, knowing this, that the trying of your faith worketh patience (Jas. 1:2-3).

My soul shall be joyful in the Lord; it shall rejoice in his salvation (Ps. 35:9).

I delight in the law of God after the inward man (Rom. 7:22).

The joy of the Lord is your strength (Neh. 8:10). Acquaint now thyself with him, and be at peace. Then shalt thou have thy delight in the Almighty, and shall lift up thy face unto God (Job 22:21, 26).

Blessed is the man that walketh not in the counsel of the ungodly (Ps. 1:1).

I shall be satisfied when I awake, with thy likeness (Ps. 17:15).

He maketh me to lie down in green pastures; he leadeth me beside the still waters (Ps. 23:2). My heart greatly rejoiceth, and with my song will I praise him (Ps. 28:7).

Thou hast turned for me my mourning into dancing (Ps. 30:11).

Delight thyself in the Lord: and he shall give thee the desires of thine heart (Ps. 37:4).

There is a river, the streams whereof shall make glad the city of God (Ps. 46:4).

If ye be reproached for the name of Christ, happy are ye (1 Pet. 4:14).

Behold, God is my salvation; I will trust, and not be afraid; for the Lord Jehovah is my strength and my song; he also is become my salvation. With joy shall ye draw water out of the wells of salvation (Isa. 12:2-3).

There is joy in the presence of the angels of God over one sinner that repenteth (Luke 15:10).

Great peace have they that love thy law; and nothing shall offend them (Ps. 119:165).

Thy words were found and I did eat them; and thy word was unto me the joy and rejoicing of mine heart (Jer. 15:16).

Well done, thou good and faithful servant; enter thou into the joy of thy Lord (Matt. 25:21). Rejoice, because your names are written in heaven (Luke 10:20).

I will praise thee with my whole heart (Ps. 138:1). My mouth shall speak the praise of the Lord (Ps. 145:21).

Is any merry? Let him sing psalms (Jas. 5:13). Behold, how good and how pleasant it is for brethren to dwell together in unity! (Ps. 133:1) It is good to sing praises unto thy name, O most High (Ps. 92:1).

Salute every saint in Jesus Christ (Phil) 4:21).

Looking unto Jesus ... who for the joy that was set before him endured the cross (Heb. 12:2).

And the peace of God, which passeth all understanding, shall keep your hearts and minds through Christ Jesus (Phil. 4:7).

Show forth the praises of him who hath called you out of darkness into his marvelous light (2 Pet. 2:9). Whether therefore ye eat, or drink, or whatsoever ye do, do all to the glory of God (1 Cor. 10:31).

I heard a great voice of much people in heaven saying, Alleluia; Salvation, and glory, and honor, and power, unto the Lord our God (Rev. 19:1).

Thou wilt keep him in perfect peace, whose mind is stayed on thee (Isa. 26:3).

In quietness and in confidence shall be your strength (Isa. 30:15).

Your joy no man taketh from you (John 16:22).

Thou shalt rejoice in every good thing which the Lord thy God hath given unto thee (Deut. 26:11).

The redeemed of the Lord shall return, and come with singing unto Zion; and everlasting joy shall be upon their heads: they shall obtain gladness and joy; and sorrow and mourning shall flee away (Isa. 51:11).

Ye shall go out with joy, and be led forth with peace; the mountains and the hills shall break forth before you into singing, and all the trees of the fields shall clap their hands (Isa. 55:12).

My servants shall sing for joy of heart ... Be ye glad and rejoice forever in that which I create: for, behold, I create Jerusalem a rejoicing, and her people a joy (Isa. 65:14, 18).

Your heart shall rejoice, and your bones shall flourish like an herb (Isa. 66:14).

Blessed are they which are persecuted for righteousness' sake ... rejoice and be exceeding glad; for great is your reward in heaven (Matt. 5:10, 12).

To be spiritually minded is life and peace (Rom. 8:6).

The kingdom of God is ... righteousness, and peace, and joy in the Holy Ghost (Rom. 14:17).

I am filled with comfort (2 Cor. 7:4).

Be filled with the Spirit; speaking to yourselves in psalms and hymns and spiritual songs, singing and making melody in your heart to the Lord (Eph. 5:18-19).

Rejoice in the Lord always ... And the peace of God, which passeth all understanding, shall keep your hearts and minds through Christ Jesus ... The God of peace shall be with you (Phil. 4:4, 7, 9).

Blessed are they which are called unto the marriage supper of the Lamb (Rev. 19:9).

I AM

I am the Lord. I change not (Mal. 3:6).

I am the Lord that healeth thee (Exod.15:26).

I AM THAT I AM (Exod. 3:14).

I am the Lord, the God of all flesh (Jer. 32:27).

I am thy salvation (Ps. 35:3).

I am thy God (Isa. 41:10).

I am God (Ps. 46:10).

I am the living bread (John 6:51).

I am the light of the world (John 8:12).

I am the way. I am the Truth. I am the Life (John 14:6).

I am the door (John 10:7).

I am the resurrection (John 11:25).

Before Abraham was, I am (John 8:58).

I am the good shepherd (John 10:14).

I am the beginning. I am the ending (Rev. 1:8).

I am the first. I am the last (Rev. 1:11).

I am he that liveth … I am alive forever more (Rev. 1:18).

What shall I do then with Jesus which is called Christ? (Matt. 27:22).

We preach not ourselves, but Christ Jesus (2 Cor. 4:5).

Remission of sins should be preached in his name (Luke 24:47).

Preaching peace by Jesus Christ: He is lord of all! (Acts 10:36).

Daily in the temple, and in every house, they ceased not to teach and preach Jesus Christ (Acts 5:42).

Philip preached Christ unto them ... Philip preached Jesus (Acts 8:5, 35).

This Jesus ... is Christ (Acts 17:3).

Jesus is the Christ (John 20:31).

Paul testified that Jesus was Christ (Acts 18:5).

Saul ... preached Christ (Acts. 9:20). Paul preached Jesus (Acts 17:18).

To us there is but one Lord Jesus Christ (1 Cor. 8:6).

Jesus Christ, the same yesterday, and today, and forever (Heb. 13:8).

Arise from the dead, and Christ shall give thee light (Eph. 5:14).

Grace and truth came by Jesus Christ (John 1:17).

Unto you is born a Saviour, which is Christ the Lord (Luke 2:11).

Put ye on the Lord Jesus Christ (Rom. 13:14).

Know ye not that Jesus Christ is in you? (2 Cor. 13:5).

There is neither male nor female; ye are all one in Christ Jesus (Gal. 3:28).

Let this mind be in you which was also in Christ Jesus (Phil. 2:5). As ye have received Jesus Christ, so walk ye in him (Col. 2:6).

Ye are Christ's and Christ is God's (1 Cor. 3:23).

All drank of that rock, and that rock was Christ (1 Cor. 10:4).

I live; yet not I, but Christ liveth in me (Gal. 2:20).

Christ is all (Col. 3:11).

The vail is done way in Christ (2 Cor. 3:14). As many as have been baptized into Christ have put on Christ (Gal. 3:27).

The head of every man is Christ (1 Cor. 11:3). We have the mind of Christ (1 Cor. 2:16).

In the name of Jesus Christ, rise up and walk (Acts 3:6).

Jesus Christ maketh thee whole: arise (Acts 9:34).

I command thee in the name of Jesus Christ to come out (Acts. 16:18).

Where two or three are gathered together in my name, there am I in the midst of them (Matt. 18:20).

Even the devils are subject unto us through thy name (Luke 10:17).

Let the word of Christ dwell in you richly (Col. 3:16). If ye be reproached for the name of Christ, happy are ye; for the spirit of glory and of God resteth upon you (1 Pet. 4:14).

Thou art the Christ of God (Luke 9:20) … joint heirs with Christ (Rom. 8:17).

Hereby know we that we dwell in him, and he in us (1 John 4:13).

I and my Father are one (John 10:30).

Henceforth, know we no man after the flesh (2 Cor. 5:16). Ye are in the Spirit, if the Spirit of God dwell in you (Rom. 8:9).

In him we live, and move, and have our being (Acts 17:28).

Christ in you (Col. 1:27).

Have ye not known? Hath it not been told you from the beginning? (Isa. 40:21).

God created man in his own image, in the image of God created he him; male and female created he them … and, behold, it was very good (Gen. 1:27, 31).

The last shall be first, and the first last (Matt. 20:16).

I in them, and thou in me, that they may be perfect in one (John 17:23).

Present every man perfect in Christ Jesus (Col. 1:28).

When that which is perfect is come, that which is in part shall be done away (1 Cor. 13:10).

And his name shall be in their foreheads (Rev. 22:4).

Behold, I make all things new (Rev. 21:5).

Glory to God in the highest, and on earth peace (Luke 2:14).

THE CITY OF OUR GOD

Come, ye blessed of my Father, inherit the kingdom prepared for you from the foundation of the world (Matt. 25:34).

In my Father's house are many mansions ... I go to prepare a place for you ... I will come again, and receive you unto myself (John 14:2-3).

And I John saw the holy city, new Jerusalem, coming down from God out of heaven, prepared as a bride adorned for her husband ... And there shall be no more death, neither sorrow, nor crying, neither shall there be any more pain ... And he carried me away in the spirit to a great and high mountain, and showed me that great city, the holy Jerusalem ... having the glory of God (Rev. 21:2, 4, 10-11).

And the street of the city was pure gold, as it were transparent glass. And I saw no temple therein: for the Lord God Almighty and the Lamb are the temple of it. And the city had no need of the sun, neither of the moon, to shine in it; for the glory of God did lighten it, and the Lamb is the light thereof. And the nations of them which are saved shall walk in the light of it: and the kings of the earth do bring their glory and honor into it ... And there shall be no night there (Rev. 21:21-25).

And they shall see his face; and his name shall be in their foreheads. They need no candle, neither light of the sun; for the Lord God giveth them light: and they shall reign forever and ever (Rev. 22:4-5).

All the ends of the world shall remember and turn unto the Lord: and all the kindreds of the nations shall worship before thee (Ps. 22:27).

Thy kingdom is an everlasting kingdom, and thy dominion endureth throughout all generations (Ps. 145:13).

The wolf shall dwell with the lamb, and the leopard shall lie down with the kid; and the calf and the young lion and the fatling together; and a little child shall lead them. And the cow and the bear shall feed; their young ones shall lie down together, and the lion shall eat straw like the ox. They shall not hurt nor destroy in all my holy mountain: for the earth shall be full of the knowledge of the Lord as the waters cover the sea (Isa. 11:6-7, 9).

The wilderness and the solitary place shall be glad for them; and the desert shall rejoice, and blossom as the rose … And the parched ground shall become a pool, and the thirsty land springs of water. And an highway shall be there, and a way, and it shall be called The way of holiness … No lion shall be there, nor any ravenous beast shall go up thereon, it shall not be found there; but the redeemed shall walk there (Isa. 35:1, 7-9).

Instead of the thorn shall come up the fir tree, and instead of the brier shall come up the myrtle tree (Isa. 55:13). Violence shall no more be heard in thy land, wasting nor destruction within thy borders; but thou shalt call thy walls Salvation, and thy gates Praise (Isa. 60:18). Behold, I create new heavens and a new earth; and the former shall not be remembered, nor come into mind (Isa. 65:17).

Thine is the kingdom, and the power, and the glory, forever (Matt. 6:13). The kingdom of heaven is at hand (Matt. 10:7). Fear not, little flock; for it is your Father's good pleasure to give you the kingdom (Luke 12:32).

And there shall be one fold, and one shepherd (John 10:16). All shall know me from the least to the greatest (Heb. 8:11).

I will rejoice in Jerusalem, and joy in my people. There shall be no more thence an infant of days, nor an old man that hath not filled his days ... And they shall build houses, and inhabit them; and they shall plant vineyards and eat the fruit of them ... and mine elect shall long enjoy the work of their hands (Isa. 65:19-22).

Neither shall a deceitful tongue be found in their mouth; for they shall feed and lie down, and none shall make them afraid (Zeph. 3:13).

All nations whom thou hast made shall come and worship before thee, O Lord; and shall glorify thy name (Ps. 86:9). All thy works shall praise thee, and thy saints shall bless thee. They shall speak of the glory of thy kingdom, and talk of thy power (Ps. 145:10-11).

And in this mountain shall the Lord make unto all people a feast of fat things ... and he will destroy in this mountain the face of the covering cast over all people, and the vail that is spread over all nations. He will swallow up death in victory (Isa. 25:6-8).

His dominion shall be from sea even to sea, and from the river even to the ends of the earth (Zech. 9:10).

In that day shall the deaf hear the words of the book, and the eyes of the blind shall see out of obscurity, and out of darkness (Isa. 29:18).

The kingdom of heaven is at hand (Matt. 3:2). My salvation shall be forever (Isa. 51:6).

Ye shall go out with joy, and be led forth with peace: the mountains and the hills shall break forth before you into singing, and all the trees of the fields shall clap their hands (Isa. 55:12).

Arise, shine; for thy light is come, and the glory of the Lord is risen upon thee (Isa. 60:1).

The Lord is in his holy temple; let all the earth keep silence before him (Hab. 2:20).

Behold, I will extend peace like a river and glory like a flowing stream (Isa. 66:12). The earth shall be filled with the knowledge of the glory of the Lord, as the waters cover the sea (Hab. 2:14). Then will I turn to the people a pure language (Zeph. 3:9).

They sung a new song, saying, Thou art worthy to take the book, and to open the seals thereof: for thou wast slain, and hast redeemed us to God by thy blood out of every kindred and tongue, and people, and nation (Rev. 5:9).

Now is come salvation, and strength, and the kingdom of our God, and the power of his Christ (Rev. 12:10). For he is Lord of lords and King of kings: and they that are with him are called, and chosen, and faithful (Rev. 17:14). And his name is called The Word of God, and on his thigh a name written, KING OF KINGS AND LORD OF LORDS (Rev. 19:13, 16).

Behold the tabernacle of God is with men, and he will dwell with them, and they shall be his people, and God himself shall be with them, and be their God (Rev. 21:3).

The King shall say, Come, ye blessed of my Father, inherit the kingdom prepared for you from the foundation of the world (Matt. 25:34).

Neither can they die any more; for they are equal unto the angels; and are the children of God, being the children of the resurrection (Luke 20:36). I give unto them eternal life (John 10:28).

There remaineth therefore a rest to the people of God (Heb. 4:9).

When that which is perfect is come, then that which is in part shall be done away (1 Cor. 13:10). When the chief

Shepherd shall appear, ye shall receive a crown of glory that fadeth not away (1 Pet. 5:4).

White robes were given unto every one of them; and it was said unto them that they should rest (Rev. 6:11). Lo, a great multitude which no man could number, of all nations, and kindreds, and people, and tongues, stood before the throne, and before the Lamb, clothed with white robes, and palms in their hands ... These are they which came out of great tribulation, and have washed their robes, and made them white in the blood of the Lamb ... They shall hunger no more, neither thirst any more ... for the Lamb shall lead them unto living fountains of waters (Rev. 7:9, 14, 16-17).

Behold, I make all things new (Rev. 21:5).

Alleluia; for the Lord God omnipotent reigneth (Rev. 19:6).

THE LAST DAYS

What shall I do with Jesus which is called Christ? (Matt. 27:22).

Take heed that no man deceive you (Matt. 24:4).

Many shall come in my name, saying, I am Christ. Take heed that ye be not deceived (Luke 21:8).

Many false prophets shall rise, and shall deceive many. If any man shall say unto you, Lo, here is Christ, or there; believe it not (Matt. 24:11, 23).

I am the Way (John 14:6). One is your Master, even Christ (Matt. 23:8). There is none other name under heaven given among men, whereby we must be saved (Acts 4:12).

No man cometh unto the Father, but by me (John 14:6). For other foundation can no man lay than that is laid, which is Jesus Christ (1 Cor. 3:11).

Ye shall hear of wars and rumors of wars: see that ye be not troubled; for all these things must come to pass, but the end is not yet. For nation shall rise against nation, and kingdom against kingdom. And then shall many be offended, and shall betray one another. And because iniquity shall abound, the love of many shall wax cold (Matt. 24:6-7, 10, 12).

Watch ye therefore (Mark 13:35).

There shall arise false Christs, and false prophets, and shall show great signs and wonders; insomuch that, if it were possible, they shall deceive the very elect (Matt. 24:24).

Call no man on earth your Master (Matt.23:9). While one saith, I am of Paul, and another, I am of Apollos; are ye not carnal? ... Therefore let no man glory in men (1 Cor. 3:4, 26).

Beware of false prophets, which come to you in sheep's clothing (Matt. 7:15). For the wisdom of this world is foolishness with God (1 Cor. 3:19).

I am the door. He that entereth not by the door into the sheepfold, but climbeth up some other way, the same is a thief and a robber (John 10:1, 9).

It is impossible but that offences will come; but woe unto him, through whom they come! (Luke 17:1)

Son of man, I have made thee a watchman unto the house of Israel: therefore hear the word at my mouth, and give them warning from me. When I say unto the wicked, Thou shalt surely die; and thou givest him not warning, nor speakest to warn the wicked from his evil way, to save his life; the same wicked man shall die in his iniquity; but his blood will I require at thine hand. Yet if thou warn the wicked, and he turn not from his wickedness, nor from his wicked way, he shall die in his iniquity; but thou hast delivered thy soul (Ezek. 3:17-19).

He that hath ears to hear, let him hear (Matt. 11:15).

Son of man, speak to the children of thy people ... If a watchman see the sword come, and blow not the trumpet, and the people be not warned; if the sword come, and take any person from among them, he is taken away in his iniquity; but his blood will I require at the watchman's hand (Ezek. 33:2, 6).

Watch ye therefore (Mark 13:35).

Little children, it is the last time: as ye have heard that antichrist shall come, even now are there many antichrists ... Whosoever denieth the Son, the same hath not the Father; but he that acknowledgeth the Son hath the Father (1 John 2:18, 23).

And every spirit that confesseth not that Jesus Christ is come in the flesh is not of God: and this is the spirit of antichrist, whereof ye have heard that it should come; and even now already is in the world (John 4:3).

The Word was made flesh, and dwelt among us ... and the Word was God (John 1:1, 14).

When the Son of man cometh, shall he find faith on the earth? (Luke 18:8). Watch, therefore, for ye know neither the day nor the hour wherein the Son of man cometh (Matt. 25:13).

Beware lest any man spoil you through philosophy and vain deceit, after the tradition of men, after the rudiments of the world, and not after Christ (Col. 2:8).

Who is God, save the Lord? And who is a rock, save our God? (2 Sam. 22:32).

False Christs and false prophets shall rise, and shall show signs and wonders, to seduce, if it were possible, even the elect (Mark 13:22) ... transforming themselves into the apostles of Christ. And no marvel; for Satan himself is transformed into an angel of light. Therefore it is no great thing if his ministers also be transformed as the ministers of righteousness; whose end shall be according to their works (2 Cor. 11:13-15).

Beloved, believe not every spirit, but try the spirits whether they are of God (1 John 4:1).

Seest thou a man wise in his own conceit? (Prov. 26:16). He that trusteth in his own heart is a fool (Prov. 28:26.

Woe unto them that are wise in their own eyes, and prudent in their own sight! (Isa. 5:21).

Not by might, nor by power, but by my Spirit, saith the Lord (Zech. 4:5). And when they had lifted up their eyes, they saw no man, save Jesus only (Matt. 17:8).

We should not trust in ourselves, but in God (2 Cor. 1:9). Take heed therefore that the light that is in thee be not darkness (Luke 11:35).

Do I seek to please men? for if I pleased men, I should not be the servant of Christ (Gal. 1:10).

Many will say to me in that day, Lord, Lord, have we not prophesied in thy name? and in thy name cast out devils? ... Depart from me, ye workers of iniquity (Matt. 7:22-23). He that entereth not by the door into the sheep-fold, but climbeth up some other way, the same is a thief and a robber (John 10:1).

Cease from thine own wisdom (Prov. 23:4).

In the latter times some shall depart from the faith (1 Tim. 4:1) ... that day shall not come, except there come a falling away first (2 Thess. 2:3).

My people hath been lost sheep: their shepherds have caused them to go astray, they have turned them away on the mountains; they have gone from mountain to hill, they have forgotten their resting place (Jer. 50:6). Return unto me, and I will return unto you, saith the Lord (Mal. 3:7).

As it shall come to pass in the last days, saith God, I will pour out my Spirit upon all flesh: and your sons and your daughters shall prophesy, and your young men shall see visions, and your old men shall dream dreams (Acts 2:17).

And the glory of the Lord shall be revealed, and all flesh shall see it together (Isa. 40:5). All flesh shall see the salvation of God (Luke 3:6).

Whosoever that forsaketh not all that he hath, he cannot be my disciple (Luke 14:33). Looking for that blessed hope, and the glorious appearing of the great God and our Saviour Jesus Christ (Tit. 2:13).

Strive to enter in at the strait gate (Luke 13:24).

It shall be in that day, that living waters shall go out from Jerusalem ... and the Lord shall be King over all the earth: in that day shall there be one Lord, and his name one (Zech. 14:8-9).

The gospel must first be published among all nations (Mark 13:10) ... that every tongue should confess that Jesus Christ is Lord (Phil. 2:11).

The gospel of the kingdom shall be preached in all the world for a witness unto all nations; and then shall the end come (Matt. 24:14).

Many shall run to and fro, and knowledge shall be increased (Dan. 12:4). Be not carried about with divers and strange doctrines (Heb. 13:9).

Avoid foolish questions, and contentions, and strivings about the law; they are unprofitable and vain (Tit. 3:9).

Why call ye me, Lord, Lord, and do not the things which I say? (Luke 6:46).

Marvel not if the world hate you (1 John 3:13). The disciple is not above his master (Matt. 10:24). The time will come when they will not endure sound doctrine, but after their own lusts shall they heap to themselves teachers, having itching ears. And they shall turn away their ears from the truth, and shall be turned unto fables (2 Tim. 3-4).

Watch.

In the last days it shall come to pass, that the mountain of the house of the Lord shall be established in the top of the mountains, and it shall be exalted above the hills; and people shall flow unto it (Mic. 4:1).

All shall know me, from the least to the greatest (Heb. 8:11).

I am Alpha and Omega, the beginning and the end, the first and the last ... I Jesus have sent mine angel to testify unto you these things in the churches. I am the bright and morning star (Rev. 22:13, 16).

Alleluia! Salvation, and glory, and honor, and power, unto the Lord our God: KING OF KINGS AND LORD OF LORDS (Rev. 19:1, 16).

DEUTERONOMY

Chapter 28

And it shall come to pass, if thou shalt hearken diligently unto the voice of the Lord thy God, to observe and to do all his commandments which I command thee this day, that the Lord thy God will set thee on high above all nations of the earth.

And all these blessings shall come on thee, and overtake thee, if thou shalt hearken unto the voice of the Lord thy God.

Blessed shalt thou be in the city, and blessed shalt thou be in the field.

Blessed shall be the fruit of thy body, and the fruit of thy ground, and the fruit of thy cattle, the increase of thy kine, and the flocks of thy sheep.

Blessed shall be thy basket and thy store.

Blessed shalt thou be when thou comest in, and blessed shalt thou be when thou goest out.

The Lord shall cause thine enemies that rise up against thee to be smitten before thy face: they shall come out against thee one way, and flee before thee seven ways.

The Lord shall command the blessing upon thee in thy storehouses, and in all that thou settest thine hand unto; and he shall bless thee in the land which the Lord thy God giveth thee.

The Lord shall establish thee an holy people unto himself, as he hath sworn unto thee, if thou shalt keep the commandments of the Lord thy God, and walk in his ways.

And all people of the earth shall see that thou art called by the name of the Lord; and they shall be afraid of thee.

And the Lord shall make thee plenteous in goods, in the fruit of thy body, and in the fruit of thy cattle, and in the fruit of thy ground, in the land which the Lord sware unto thy fathers to give thee.

The Lord shall open unto thee his good treasure, the heaven to give the rain unto thy land in his season, and to bless all the work of thine hand: and thou shalt lend unto many nations, and thou shalt not borrow.

And the Lord shall make thee the head, and not the tail; and thou shalt be above only, and thou shalt not be beneath; if that thou hearken unto the commandments of the Lord thy God, which I command thee this day, to observe and to do them.

And thou shalt not go aside from any of the words which I command thee this day, to the right hand, or to the left, to go after other gods to serve them.

THE 91ST PSALM

He that dwelleth in the secret place of the most High shall abide under the shadow of the Almighty.

I will say of the Lord, he is my refuge and my fortress: my God; in him will I trust.

Surely he shall deliver thee from the snare of the fowler, and from the noisome pestilence. He shall cover thee with his feathers, and under his wings shalt thou trust; his truth shall be thy shield and buckler.

Thou shalt not be afraid for the terror by night; nor for the arrow that flieth by day. Nor for the pestilence that walketh in darkness; nor for the destruction that wasteth at noonday.

A thousand shall fall at thy side, and ten thousand at thy right hand; but it shall not come nigh thee.

Only with thine eyes shalt thou behold and see the reward of the wicked.

Because thou hast made the Lord, which is my refuge, even the most High, thy habitation; there shall no evil befall thee, neither shall any plague come nigh thy dwelling.

For he shall give his angels charge over thee, to keep thee in all thy ways. They shall bear thee up in their hands, lest thou dash thy foot against a stone.

Thou shalt tread upon the lion and adder; the young lion and the dragon shalt thou trample under feet..

Because he hath set his love upon me, therefore will I deliver him: I will set him on high, because he hath known my name.

He shall call upon me, and I will answer him; I will be with him in trouble; I will deliver him, and honor him. With long life will I satisfy him, and show him my salvation.

LUKE

Chapter 15

Then drew near unto him all the publicans and sinners for to hear him. And the Pharisees and scribes murmured, saying, This man receiveth sinners, and eateth with them.

And he spake this parable unto them, saying, What man of you, having an hundred sheep, if he lose one of them, doth not leave the ninety and nine in the wilderness, and go after that which is lost, until he find it? And when he hath found it, he layeth it on his shoulders, rejoicing. And when he cometh home, he calleth together his friends and neighbors, saying unto them, Rejoice with me; for I have found my sheep which was lost.

I say unto you, that likewise joy shall be in heaven over one sinner that repenteth, more than over ninety and nine just persons, which need no repentance.

Either what woman having ten pieces of silver, if she lose one piece, doth not light a candle, and sweep the house, and seek diligently till she find it? And when she hath found it, she calleth her friends and her neighbors together, saying, Rejoice with me; for I have found the piece which I had lost.

Likewise, I say unto you, there is joy in the presence of the angels of God over one sinner that repenteth.

And he said, a certain man had two sons: And the younger of them said to his father, Father, give me the portion of goods that falleth to me. And he divided unto them his living.

And not many days after, the younger son gathered all together, and took his journey into a far country, and there wasted his substance with riotous living. And when he had spent all, there arose a mighty famine in that land; and he began to be in want.

And he went and joined himself to a citizen of that country; and he sent him into his fields to feed swine. And he would fain have filled his belly with the husks that the swine did eat; and no man gave unto him.

And when he came to himself, he said, How many hired servants of my father's have bread enough and to spare, and I perish with hunger! I will arise and go to my father, and will say unto him, Father, I have sinned against heaven, and before thee, and am no more worthy to be called thy son: make me as one of thy hired servants.

And he arose, and came to his father. But when he was yet a great way off, his father saw him, and had compassion, and ran, and fell on his neck, and kissed him.

And the son said unto him, Father, I have sinned against heaven, and in thy sight, and am no more worthy to be called thy son.

But the father said to his servants, Bring forth the best robe, and put it on him; and put a ring on his hand, and shoes on his feet: And bring hither the fatted calf, and kill it; and let us eat, and be merry: For this, my son, was dead, and is alive again; he was lost, and is found. And they began to be merry.

Now his elder son was in the field: and as he came and drew nigh to the house, he heard music and dancing. And he called one of the servants, and asked what these things meant.

And he said unto him, Thy brother is come; and thy father hath killed the fatted calf, because he hath received him safe and sound.

And he was angry, and would not go in: therefore came his father out, and entreated him.

And he, answering, said to his father, Lo, these many years do I serve thee, neither transgressed I at any time thy commandment; and yet thou never gavest me a kid, that I might make merry with my friends: But as soon as this thy son was come, which hath devoured thy living with harlots, thou hast killed for him the fatted calf.

And he said unto him, Son, thou art ever with me, and all that I have is thine. It was meet we should make merry, and be glad: for this thy brother was dead, and is alive again; and was lost, and is found.

JOHN

Chapter 14

Let not your heart be troubled: ye believe in God, believe also in me.

In my Father's house are many mansions: if it were not so, I would have told you. I go to prepare a place for you. And if I go and prepare a place for you, I will come again, and receive you unto myself; that where I am, there ye may be also. And whither I go ye know, and the way ye know.

Thomas saith unto him, Lord, we know not whither thou goest; and how can we know the way? Jesus saith unto him, I am the way, and the truth, and the life: no man cometh unto the Father, but by me. If ye had known me, ye should have known my Father also: and from henceforth ye know him, and have seen him.

Philip saith unto him, Lord, shew us the Father, and it sufficeth us. Jesus saith unto him, Have I been so long time with you, and yet hast thou not known me, Philip? He that hath seen me hath seen the Father; and how sayest thou then, Shew us the Father? Believest thou not that I am in the Father, and the Father in me? The words that I speak unto you I speak not of myself: but the Father that dwelleth in me, he doth the works.

Believe me that I am in the Father, and the Father in me: or else believe me for the very works' sake.

Verily, verily, I say unto you, He that believeth on me, the works that I do shall he do also; and greater works than these shall he do; because I go unto my Father. And whatsoever ye shall ask in my name, that will I do, that the Father may be glorified in the Son. If ye shall ask anything in my name, I will do it.

If ye love me, keep my commandments. And I will pray the Father, and he shall give you another Comforter, that he may abide with you forever. Even the Spirit of truth; whom the world cannot receive, because it seeth him not, neither knoweth him: but ye know him; for he dwelleth with you, and shall be in you.

I will not leave you comfortless: I will come unto you. Yet a little while, and the world seeth me no more; but ye see me: because I live, ye shall live also.

At that day ye shall know that I am in my Father, and ye in me, and I in you.

He that hath my commandments, and keepeth them, he it is that loveth me: and he that loveth me shall be loved of my Father, and I will love him, and will manifest myself to him.

Judas saith unto him, not Iscariot, Lord, how is it that thou wilt manifest thyself unto us, and not unto the world? Jesus answered and said unto him, If a man love me, he will keep my words; and my Father will love him, and we will come unto him, and make our abode with him.

He that loveth me not keepeth not my sayings: and the word which ye hear is not mine, but the Father's which sent me. These things have I spoken unto you being yet present with you.

But the Comforter, which is the Holy Ghost, whom the Father will send in my name, he shall teach you all things, and bring all things to your remembrance, whatsoever I have said unto you.

Peace I leave with you, my peace I give unto you: not as the world giveth, give I unto you. Let not your heart be troubled, neither let it be afraid. Ye have heard how I said unto you, I go away, and come again unto you. If ye loved me, ye would rejoice, because I said, I go unto the Father: for my Father is greater than I. And now I have told you before it come to pass, that, when it is come to pass, ye might believe.

Hereafter I will not talk much with you: for the prince of this world cometh, and hath nothing in me. But that the world may know that I love the Father; and as the Father gave me commandment, even so I do. Arise, let us go hence.

HIGH WATCH

Look unto me, and be ye saved, all the ends of the earth (Isa. 45:22).

At that day shall a man *look* to his Maker (Isa. 17:7).

Look, ye blind, that ye may see (Isa. 42:18).

Look to the rock whence ye are hewn (Isa. 51:1).

Jesus made him *look up,* and he was restored (Mark 8:25).

To them that *look* for him shall he appear (Heb. 9:28).

Look for new heavens and a new earth, wherein dwelleth righteousness (2 Pet. 3:13).

I *looked* and, behold, a door was opened (Rev. 4:1).

Lift up your eyes. and *look* on the fields; for they are white already to harvest (John 4:35).

Whoso *looketh* into the perfect law of liberty, and contin-ueth therein ... shall be blessed (Jas. 1:25).

They bring unto him one that is deaf ... and *looking up* to heaven, he saith unto him ... be opened (Mark 7:34).

Lift up your heads; for your redemption draweth nigh (Luke 21:28).

Lift up thy face unto God (Job 22:26).

Lift up thy voice with strength (Isa. 40:9).

I will *lift up* mine eyes unto the hills (Ps. 121:1).

And they *lifted up* their eyes, and saw the ark (1 Sam. 6:13).

And David *lifted up* his eyes, and saw the angel (1 Chron. 21:16).

I Nebuchadnezzar *lifted up* mine eyes unto heaven, and my understanding returned unto me (Dan. 4:34).

Jesus *lifted up* his eyes, and said, Father, I thank thee that thou hast heard me (John 11:41).

Lift up your eyes ... and behold (Isa. 40:26).

I, if I be *lifted up* from the earth, will draw all men unto me (John 12:32).

And when they had *lifted up* their eyes, they saw no man, save Jesus only (Matt. 17:8).

As Moses *lifted up* the serpent in the wilderness, even so must the Son of man be *lifted up* (John 3:14).

The light of the body is the *eye* (Matt. 6:22).

He cometh ... and every *eye* shall see him (Rev. 1:7).

Lord, open his *eyes* that he may *see* (2 Kings 6:17).

The righteous *see* it, and are glad (Job 22:19).

The humble shall *see*, and be glad (Ps. 69:32).

Thine eyes shall *see* the King in his beauty (Isa. 33:17).

The man of wisdom shall *see* thy name (Mic. 6:9).

Blessed are the pure in heart, for they shall *see* God (Matt. 5:8).

What went ye out into the wilderness to *see*? (Matt. 11:7).

And they shall *see* his face; and his name shall be in their foreheads (Rev. 22:4).

Go, set a watchman, let him declare what he *seeth* (Isa. 21:6).

Watch!

Watch and pray!

Watch ye, stand fast in the faith ... be strong (1 Cor. 16:13).

Watch thou in all things ... do the work of an evangelist, make full proof of thy ministry (2 Tim. 4:5).

Blessed is he that *watcheth* (Rev. 16:15).

Blessed are those whom the Lord when he cometh shall find *watching* (Luke 12:37).

What I say unto you I say unto all, *watch*! (Mark 13:37).

JESUS CHRIST'S WORD

After His Resurrection

All hail! (Matt. 28:9).

Be not afraid! (Matt. 28:10).

Ought not Christ to have suffered these things, and to enter into his glory? (Luke 26:36).

Peace be unto you (Luke 24:36).

Why are ye troubled? and why do thoughts arise in your hearts? ... It behooved Christ to suffer, and to rise from the dead the third day; that repentance and remission of sins should be preached in his name among all nations (Luke 24:38, 46-47).

Go ye into all the world and preach the gospel to every creature (Mark 16:15).

And these signs shall follow them that believe; in my name shall they cast out devils; they shall speak with new tongues; they shall take up serpents; and if they drink any deadly thing, it shall not hurt them; they shall lay hands on the sick, and they shall recover (Mark 16:17-18).

Blessed are they which have not seen, and yet have believed (John 20:29).

Follow me (John 21:19).

Children, have ye any meat? ... Cast the net on the right side of the ship, and ye shall find ... Bring of the fish which ye have now caught ... Come and dine (John 21:5-6, 10, 12).

Lovest thou me? ... Feed my lambs (John 21:17).

All power is given unto me in heaven and in earth (Matt. 28:18).

Go ye therefore, and teach all nations, baptizing them in the name of the Father, and of the Son, and of the Holy Ghost; teaching them to observe all things whatsoever I have commanded you. Lo, I am with you alway, even unto the end of the world (Matt. 28:19-20).

Behold, I send the promise of my Father upon you; but tarry ye in the city of Jerusalem, until ye be endued with power from on high (Luke 24:49).

Ye shall receive power, after that the Holy Ghost is come upon you; and ye shall be witnesses unto me ... and unto the uttermost part of the earth (Acts 1:8).

JESUS CHRIST

The Finisher: Looking unto Jesus the finisher of our faith (Heb. 12:2). I have finished the work thou gavest me to do (John 17:4).

The Deliverer: He hath sent me ... to preach deliverance ... to set at liberty them that are bruised (Luke 4:18).

The Victor: I have the keys of hell and of death (Rev. 1:18).

The Conqueror: I have overcome the world (John 16:33).

Only Foundation: Other foundation can no man lay than ... Jesus Christ (1 Cor. 3:11).

The Propitiation: And he is the propitiation for our sins; and not for ours only, but also for the sins of the whole world (1 John 2:2).

The Mediator: Jesus the mediator of the new covenant (Heb. 12:24).

The Saviour: Him hath God exalted to be a Prince and Saviour (Acts 5:31).

The Redeemer: Thou hast redeemed us to God (Rev. 5:9).

The Shepherd: I am the good shepherd (John 10:14).

The King: He is KING OF KINGS (Rev. 19:16).

The Way: I am the way (John 14:6).

The Teacher: Then opened he their understanding, that they might understand the scriptures (Luke 24:45).

The Master: Ye call me Master ... for so I am (John 13:13).

The Light: I am the light of the world (John 8:12).

The Lord: The second man is the Lord from heaven (1 Cor. 15:47).

The Unchanging: Jesus Christ the same yesterday, and today, and forever (Heb. 13:8).

The Companion: I will never leave thee, nor forsake thee (Heb. 13:5).

The Lover: I have loved you (John 13:34).

The Holy One: Thou art the Holy One of God (Mark 1:24).

The True God: This is the true God and eternal life (1 John 5:20).

The Word: The Word was made flesh, and dwelt among us (John 1:14).

The Physician: Come unto me ... and I will give you rest (Matt. 11:28).

The Christ: Jesus is the Christ (John 20:31).

The Ransom: Who gave himself a ransom for all (1Tim. 2:6).

Son of God: Of a truth thou art the Son of God (Matt. 14:33).

God: And the Word was God (John 1:1).

THE PRAYERS OF
JESUS CHRIST

When he had sent the multitude away, he went up into a mountain apart to pray (Matt. 14:23).

And in the morning, rising up a great while before day, he went out and departed into a solitary place, and there prayed (Mark 1:35).

He continued all night in prayer (Luke 6:12).

It came to pass, as he was alone praying, his disciples were with him (Luke 9:18).

As he was praying in a certain place, when he ceased, one of his disciples said unto him, Lord, teach us to pray (Luke 11:1).

And he withdrew himself into the wilderness, and prayed (Luke 5:16).

Jesus being baptized, and praying, the heaven was opened (Luke 3:21).

As he prayed, the fashion of his countenance was altered, and his raiment was white and glistening (Luke 9:29).

He kneeled down and prayed ... and being in agony he prayed more earnestly (Luke 22:41, 44).

I thank thee, O Father, because thou hast hid these things from the wise and prudent, and hast revealed them unto babes (Matt. 11:25).

Father, I thank thee that thou hast heard me. And I know that thou hearest me always (John 11:41-42).

Father, glorify thy name (John 12:28).

Father, the hour is come; glorify thy Son (John 17:1). Glorify thou me ... with the glory which I had with thee before the world was (John 17:5).

Father, if it be possible, let this cup pass from me; nevertheless not as I will, but as thou wilt (Matt. 26:39).

Father, forgive them; for they know not what they do (Luke 23:34).

Father, into thy hands I commend my spirit (Luke 23:46).

THE LORD'S PRAYER

The Prayer of Our Lordship

Recognition: Our Father which art in heaven, hallowed be thy name.

Spirit's Commands: Thy kingdom come. Thy will be done on earth as it is in heaven. Give us this day our daily bread. Forgive us our debts, as we forgive our debtors. Lead us not into temptation. Deliver us from evil.

Recognition: Thine is the kingdom, and the power, and the glory, forever.

THE LESSON OF PETER

His Fall

Peter, sleepest thou? Couldest not thou watch one hour? (Mark 14:37).

Peter smote the high priest's servant, and cut off his right ear (John 18:10).

And Peter followed afar off (Luke 22:54).

Peter sat with the servants, and warmed himself at the fire (Mark 14:54).

One of the maids ... looked upon him and said, And thou also wast with Jesus of Nazareth (Mark 14:66-67).

But he denied before them all, saying, I know not what thou sayest (Matt. 26:70).

He began to curse and swear, saying, I know not this man of whom ye speak (Mark 14:71).

Remembering the words of Jesus, he went out, and wept bitterly (Matt. 26:75).

THE LESSON OF PETER

His Victory

Jesus said unto Peter the third time, Simon, son of Jonas, lovest thou me? And he said, Lord, thou knowest that I love thee. Jesus said, Feed my sheep (John 21:17).

Tarry ye in the city of Jerusalem, until ye be endued with power from on high (Luke 24:49).

They went up into an upper room, where abode Peter ... and they continued with one accord in prayer and supplication (Acts 1:13-14).

And they were all filled with the Holy Ghost (Acts 2:4) and Peter lifted up his voice, and said unto them, Repent, and be baptized, every one of you in the name of Jesus Christ for the remission of sins, and ye shall receive the gift of the Holy Ghost. ... And with many other words did he testify and exhort. Then they that gladly received his word were baptized; and the same day there were added unto them about three thousand souls (Acts 2:14, 38, 40-41).

A certain man lame from his mother's womb was carried ... and Peter said, In the name of Jesus Christ of Nazareth rise up and walk. And he took him by the right hand and lifted him up; and immediately his feet and ankle bones received strength (Acts 3:2, 6-7).

Then Peter, filled with the Holy Ghost, said, Be it known unto you all, that by the name of Jesus Christ, whom ye crucified, whom God raised from the dead, even by him doth this man stand here before you whole (Acts 4:10).

And believers were the more added to the Lord, multitudes both of men and women (Acts 5:14).

THE NEW BIRTH

Come: Him that cometh to me I will in no wise cast out (John 6:37).

Repent: If we confess our sins, he is faithful and just to forgive us our sins, and to cleanse us from all unrighteousness (1 John 1:9).

Believe: If thou canst believe, all things are possible (Mark 9:23).

Abide: Abide in me (John 15:4).

Forgive: Forgive, and ye shall be forgiven (Luke 6:37).

Love: Love one another as I have loved you (John 13:34).

Receive: As many as received him, to them gave he power to become the sons of God (John 1:12).

Confess: Whosoever shall confess me before men, him will I confess also before my Father which is in heaven (Matt. 10:32).

Teach: Teach all nations ... all things whatsoever I have commanded you (Matt. 28:19-20).

Heal: Heal the sick (Matt. 10:8).

Pray: Men ought always to pray (Luke 18:1).

Look: Unto them that look for him shall he appear (Heb. 9:28).

Watch: I say unto all, Watch (Mark 13:37).

Tarry: Tarry ye ... until ye be endued with power from on high (Luke 24:49).

COME

Come unto me (Matt. 11:28).

Come unto me and drink (John 7:37).

Come and take (Rev. 22:17).

Come forth (John 11:43).

Come after me (Mark 8:34).

Come and see (John 1:39).

Come ye blessed (Matt. 25:34).

Come take up the cross (Mark 8:34).

Come and dine (John 21:12).

KEEP

If ye love me, keep my commandments (John 14:15).

Keep the unity of the Spirit (Eph. 4:3).

Keep unspotted from the world (Jas. 1:27).

Keep yourselves in the love of God (Jude 21).

Keep the faith (2 Tim. 4:7).

Keep thyself pure (1Tim. 5:22).

Keep yourselves from idols (1 John 5:21).

Keep the heart diligently (Prov. 4:23).

Keep thy tongue from evil (Ps. 34:13).

Keep my words (John 14:23).

ABOUT THE AUTHOR

Lillian DeWaters was born in 1883 and lived in Stamford, Connecticut. She grew up with a Christian Science background and in her early teens began to study metaphysics and on that same day to seriously study the Bible. "It was from the Bible that I learned to turn from all else to God direct …. What stood out to me above all else was the fact presented, that when they turned to God they received Light and Revelation; they walked and talked with God; and they found peace and freedom."

She published a few books while actively within the Christian Science organization, and then in 1924 she had an awakening experience when it was as though a veil was parted and Truth was revealed to her. From that point she began to receive numerous unfoldments which led to her separation from the Christian Science organization.

She created her own publishing company and wrote over 30 books published in 15 languages. She was well-known as a teacher and healer throughout the world.

All of her books were written based on her direct unfoldments of Absolute Truth.